Tears

of the

Wolf Moon

by James Clarke-Coley

First Published: November 2025
by
Budding Authors Assistant
www.help2publish.co.uk

ISBN: 9781917128223

INTRODUCTION

The poems in *Tears of the Wolf Moon* are both a love letter and an alarm bell, to the beauty I have witnessed in my work as a guardian of the UK rivers. I write these poems beside the river, where kingfishers and otters played freely, now they have dwindled to a thread of their former abundance.

The collection is not a lament but a celebration to the wonder I have witnessed - the particular curiosity in a hare's eye, the resonance of birdsong and the luminous colouring of a brook trout. It is a witness statement, a field notebook written in verse, and - most urgently - a legacy for my grandchildren. I have measured water quality, counted fish losses and reported on pollution, but poetry can describe what complex data, and the camera cannot capture.

The poems chronicle the beauty I have witnessed and document the losses I have seen - because they must not be forgotten. I have also included verse on the alternative sides of human nature, because we are part of the living world too.

To grandchildren and all who will inherit this diminished but still wonderous world, I leave you these verses as both an elegy and a plea - know what lived here - know what we lost - and know it's not too late to choose a different path.

DEDICATION

I dedicate this anthology of verse to the selfless volunteers who work tirelessly to protect and preserve our wildlife, plants and rivers.

WILDLIFE POEMS FOR FIRESIDE READS

Animal Blues

Tears of the Wolf Moon

CONTENTS

Reflections

Dwindling Legacy?

Dwindling Legacy?

James Clarke-Coley has a keen sense of rhythm, and this lends itself to the natural world in so many ways. Each title is carefully chosen by the poet, for its humour or pathos, each one thought-provoking to entice you to read the corresponding poem.

Clarke-Coley applies his comprehensive knowledge of nature and wildlife to bring their stories alive and in so doing, confronts us with the reality of their plight, and the predicament animals find themselves in often due to the ignorance of humans. By personifying the creatures, he gives them a voice. In Chameleon Superhero, the narrator is a chameleon who speaks of the end of the world and a warning to humankind with the final question. In addition to this, his descriptions of their movements – actions and reactions – captures their very essence. In *What a Spectacle*, the poet uses sibilance, 'slithering, sibilant, silent serpent' to demonstrate the snakes' actions. He evokes the dangers and demonstrates that killing of prey is necessary to keep offspring and themselves alive with food. In the poem, *A Vixen's Scream*, the line, 'In my bloodlust I kill the living... I am Vixen; the unforgiving' shocks us but it reveals this inherent need for animals to sustain themselves.

Clarke-Coley adapts legends and stories to depict his animals. In *Ratty Comes Home*, there are references to *The Wind in the Willows*. In *What Don't We Understand*, he hints at the legend of Prince Llywelyn where he kills his faithful dog, Gelert because he thinks he has attacked his son. He then sees this is not the case and just like the wolf in the poem has helped save the child. The powerful line, "Kill to survive, but your heart must care" reminds us of how much we owe the animal kingdom.

Analogies and metaphors abound throughout allowing us to visualise the images of wildlife. In *Bat Out of Hell*, we see the mention of 'Soprano', 'Madama' and 'Puccini's operatic aria' in describing the sounds of the bats. In *Eight-legged Seamstress*, the spider becomes 'a venomous tailor' and wraps her victims in a 'silken funeral shroud.'

I have thoroughly enjoyed reading James Clarke-Coley's poetry and I am honoured to comment on them. I am sure you will enjoy reading them and perusing the exquisite language he adopts to demonstrate not just the plight of our wildlife but the sheer magnificence and beauty of the natural world. I will leave you with a phrase from *Where Have all the Wasps Gone?* If we do not have those 'darned things', pollination will be affected, and human life may become extinct. We are all part of the natural world and must take care of it. These poems help us to celebrate the magnificence of nature.

E M Tilstone

Author of *Hearsay*

TEARS OF THE WOLF MOON

Orange moonlight floods crystal eve,
Alpha's senses shine so bright.
Time to hunt, cries terrified trees,
snout raised slow to the perfumed night.
Prey's scent floods on darkening breeze,
frost-reddened maples, bid geese to leave.

Alpha hunts alone, his pack naïve,
youngsters' maturity hasn't flowered.
King still commands these surly dukes,
slinking worship, raised hackles, cowered.
Sullen, but quake at his sharp rebuke,
who knows what they believe?

Cruel, yellowed, Asiatic eyes,
Beta, she who must be obeyed.
Regal bearing, for all to see,
fierce warrior queen, unafraid.
King looks on – Oh! for her he'd die
Bore his whelps, bends her knee.

Quiver; deer, caribou or quail,
feels their soft scent against his face.
Leaping rush in a deadly flow,

his silky crouching gait at pace.
Loves soft flesh of a white-tailed doe,
rules supreme on his kingdom trail.

Life is crushed; and so too the fear,
shrouded wolf moon sheds no tear.

A Vixen's Scream

I hear rustling beneath decayed debris,
welcome velvet touch of slow rising breeze.
Tiptoe through my secret woodland trees,
vole's errant children mean sweet prey to me.

Sweet sage, broom and magenta claw,
scents of fragrant forest pervade my brain.
Hear woodpecker's hammered refrain,
echoed rat-tat at the churchyard door.

Invisible, wind-cloaked huntress.
scruff hairs bristle, senses awake,
Avenging angel to all who quake,
oblivious to their tame distress.

Black ankle stockings leave no trace,
carefully measured silken tread.
Sound, absorbed by a hollow space,
instinct, no naive rush ahead.

Carnage site of blood and gore.
In my bloodlust I kill the living,
I am Vixen; the unforgiving!
Bright eyes strewn on the forest floor.

Heard him scream, I will let him wait,
my hunger sated, I feel another.
Jack to my Jill, should I bother?
I'll decide when we mate.

Smelt his male musk overwhelm me,
last night in the garden stealing scraps.
He walked towards me, ears pinned back,
I spat; cold eyes reject his plea.

My bitter loneliness I too extol,
hear his harrowed scream tonight.
Come my Prince in guarded sight,
give me motherhood, ease my soul.

BAT OUT OF HELL

Pipistrelle hunts dusking field,
Sonar directed; Eyes not peeled.
Insects fluttering, balmy night,
fatally, now realised their plight.

Soprano cousin without a hitch,
Madama's highest, at fever pitch.
Puccini operatic aria floats,
on butterflies fluttering requiem notes.

Hang upside down for coming day,
in rotting belfry hang and sway.
Their protection saves our dwelling,
from developer's wallet swelling.

Vampire bat's scary rictus leer,
flying insects cower with fear.
Silver black phantom moonlit night,
as tolled bell brings devil's light.

Raucously roost in tree lined sprawl.
flying foxes now rest their bones.
Noisy nightly winged withdrawal,
to fast food diner jungle zones.

Only mammal really flying.
Not beaten for want of trying.
Gliding squirrel, or monkey swing,
best left to the patagium wing.

Creatures modelled man's first flight,
no carbon footprint left in sight.
Swoop the faded nighttime air,
to roost in demon's darkened lair.

WHAT A SPECTACLE

Apep and Wadjet lovers coiled.
Goddess and King entwine.
Egyptians even built a shrine,
regal Cobras tempers boiled.

Wadjet regaled hissing dread,
'Apep make your subjects kneel.
You must earn your royal seal,
bring me back a mongoose head'

Slithering, sibilant, silent serpent,
spectacled hooded, terror twisted.
Jungle evening humid misted,
whispered satin scaly descent.

On the quiet leaf mould floor,
stillness, calms and senses prey.
Scurrying rodent unaware, blasé,
woven scents, tracks and spoor.

Stalking lace brushed the grass,
King Apep hears no courtier's simper.
Only his subjects whine and whimper,
tremulous at the regal pass.

One sleek discordant string,
brindled, grizzly long and slim.
Cobra's venom doesn't bother him,
Rikki hunts the hunter king.

Rodent's prey's last breath, 'I bring,
greetings from the slim snake charmer'.
Perplexed cobra, frozen karma,
awaiting nemesis, fear takes wings.

Mongoose appears; no escape,
as snake flexes his poison gland.
Proud King and the pretender stand,
spitting venomous fangs agape.

Cobra strikes, empty space,
shift in time and blur of light
His skull is cracked, one fatal bite,
frozen smile on his dead face.

Jungle breathes collective sigh,
raucous movement starts again.
Wadjet spits revengeful pain,
mongoose better learn to fly.

OLD SALTIE

Survived from primordial slime,
furnace heat, rest to cool.
Water warm but blood ice cold,
hides in mud, until ambush time.
Grab drinkers at your pool,
instinct driven centuries old.

Sun sears pastel colours live,
belly moves heart-saving slow.
You're joking Crocodile Dundee
wrestle Saltie, you don't survive.
Never let your real fear show.
to a one-ton reptile you cannot flee.

Hissing, chirrups, growling roar,
many sounds to warn a foe,
But not when wary at the pool,
Quiet; when food is at the door.
Drags intruder down below,
in her deathroll, scaley ghoul.

Sixth extinction now to try,
King survivor wears a crown,
like aged T Rex lying down,
nearest link to times gone by.

Listens for chirrups anew,

huge great jaws and tiny legs.

Supports her weight over precious eggs,

reptilian mum, last of the few.

THE DIE IS CAST?

Far away from modern strife,
who could really know your worth?
Aerate soil, loam the fields,
Oh, humble heroine of life.
Don't hide your light in darkened earth,
work to grow the farmer's yield.

Our world's gardens are truly blessed,
release the songbirds' winter cold.
Blind moles love your soft caress,
feed the regal robins' nest.
Hedgehogs search every cast and mould,
not for them the slugs and snails.

A world without you...

Lost ferns won't sway in summer breeze,
flowers neither bloom nor please.
Meadows absent for the plover,
no soft shade for a lover.

Forest glades bloom desert black,
callous weeds still dying back.
Hillsides crumble to barren land,
no lakeside reeds left to stand.

Think, when meadows and rivers die,
birds no longer sing on high.
What must happen to all mankind,
if there's nothing left behind.

Arise, emerge from your dark home,
don't hide your light in the loam.
Let's cherish a world you allow,
modest earthworms take a bow.

WHERE HAVE ALL THE WASPS GONE?

Black and yellow, stinging tail,
drawn to the fruit and bush.
Ensuring one more sugar rush,
bees in the hive, beware no sale.

Children crying, throbbing finger.
grab a handy insecticide spray.
Surely, that stripey pest must pay,
for spoiled party if they linger.

Greenfly and milling aphids shirk,
barren vines no grapes to rear.
Black and yellow sommelier,
toasting those little devil's work.

This summer no wasps pay homage,
BBQ held, devoid of stings.
No parents' cries of 'Those darned things',
electric swatter placed in storage.

Will we cope with the dwindling few,
reducing world plant pollination.
Feeding, feeding a hungry nation,
better not poison the mackerel too.

RATTY COMES HOME

Evil alerts her killer's lust,
water vole gone but seek she must.
Silky mink goes on her way,
tracking any other prey.

Visits moorhen's nest instead,
eats the young, leaves parents dead.
Stronger musk crinkles her nose,
enters the trap, feels it close.

Water vole now reappearing,
a 'plop' before disappearing.
Diving tunnels in the far bank,
pike and buzzard will draw a blank.

Glances warily over his shoulder,
quietly slips from the boulder.
No hesitation; where to hide,
an instinct resonates inside

Ratty, never look back in fear,
minks' long cruel reign is ended here.
Make your tunnels, otters can't see,
you're home again happy and free.

Our bankside thistle bends and blows,
angler hears welcome 'plop' and knows.
Sleek, silvery head sweeps on past,
his river friend is home at last.

Mink now expelled invasive pest,
red crayfish, mitten crab the rest.
Ratty the hero, going home,
another cuckoo's nest has flown.

WEASLEY RECOGNISED BUT
STOATLY DIFFERENT

Terrified screams pierce the morn,
chills a night for a bleaker dawn.
A giant fallen to Tom Thumb,
Goliath, Cyclops had never won.

Stoat swiftly dispatches hare,
now, appears nervous, aware.
Mussel twitches crimson splattered,
his victor's crown never flattered.

A weasel cousin stands his ground,
he always was a cheeky hound.
'How did you manage to survive,
fighting something five times your size?'

'You are my cousin,' said the Stoat,
'But touch that hare, I'll have your throat'
Weasel's hunt had taken its toll,
'Give me a leg and swap my vole'.

'Now clear off you cheeky beggar,
her indoors, certainly have yer!
When my girl Jill gets her goat,
you'll wish you'd never seen a stoat'.

Weasel didn't see tomorrow,
angry Jill streaks from her burrow.
Killed poor weasel with one cruel bite,
he didn't have a chance to fight.

'Now stick this one in the larder,
you'll really have to be much harder.
I've got a home and five kits to keep,
you were too soft on that sad creep.

Spotted a warbler's nest nearby,
steal a couple of eggs to try.
You'd better make it quite a few,
or you'll be in the larder too'.

Snakes and Adders

Black and brown diamond patterned neat,
camouflaged in the dying day.
Tongue flicks, senses that febrile heat,
of scented musk of mouse at play.

Laying ambush in dying light,
shy, in a world so sadly shunned.
Stays quiet, keeping out of sight,
sudden strike, careless rodent stunned,

Neat urban gardens not her place,
danger in the steel wire and net.
Not seen often in human space,
but fleeing mouse made her forget.

Venom fangs, little human harm,
without her, rodents wreck the farm.

WEASEL ON THE WARPATH

Missing black tip on her tail,
not a stoat in winter gear.
Follows errant rodent trail,
she smells the snivelling fear.

Slips through the dew-stained path,
careful; rat is not alone.
Coiled grass snake in striking wrath,
weasel enters killing zone.

Scene unfolds, now there's three,
cowardly rat, cannot hide.
Two hunters in rivalry,
victors, how will they decide?

Weasel sudden turn and leap,
runs, jumps, pirouetting play.
Rat transfixed, snake retreat,
Mesmerising display.

Hear those hideous rodent wails,
weasel War Dance never fails.

CHAMELEON SUPERHERO

Die tonight or be immortal?
Am I tired of this world, perhaps?
60 million years, seen it all.
After me, will the world collapse?

I'm super but not a hero,
unseen as watching from a tree.
Move to a leaf I'm also zero,
my first power, invisibility.

My special eyes, mean I can hide,
in my Madagascan jungle lair.
Seems like I have eyes in my backside,
my prey seems blissfully unaware.

Climbing branches, I stick like glue,
zygodactyl feet, prehensile tail.
My third superpower is hardly new,
sticky long tongue will never fail.

Still toying with the conundrum broached,
the earth implodes, it's quite insane.
Floating in a galaxy encroached,
even black holes can't end my pain.

As countless lovers, families, friends subside,
well, as a human what would you decide?

WHAT DON'T WE UNDERSTAND?

Felt unknown longing in his soul,
world's peace was not his own,
once tall grass, now stiff sentry fronds,
horizon draws his gaze.
Crystalised sugar, chiffon thin,
reflects his ancestral pain.

Snow sparkled, scattered by the Gods,
on some casual whim.
Aching virginal white, soiled by,
bloody tracks' scarlet stain.
Once more that soft anguished moan,
crouched, sees his dying prey.

Now the hunters butcher the beast,
caribou hind means life.
Bury meat, the rest to carry,
ensures his clan survives,
Sensing other beings afar,
vanish into the mist,

Family greets them back alive,
more smaller mouths to feed.

Buried meat for the young to grow.
Farewells: returned at speed.
Over ferocious ice melt stream,
met slope at steadfast run.

Silence broken by child-like scream,
sees a boy in the flow,
His greatest enemy's sole heir,
but must save the child's life.
Ancestral code 'Kill to survive,
but your heart must care'.

Leapt bravely into icy flow,
fought the raging current.
Slumped on shore, the worst had passed.
Wracked cough, the boy still breathed,
Relieved, he stretched, shook and rose,
A shot rang out; no pain.

A man strode to clutch his boy close,
kicked the carcass where it lay.
A boy and wolf in strange caress.
he viewed them from above.
Certain, as blood bloomed on the ground,
new Alpha for his pack.

DRAGON'S THRONE

Blood-riders on the sea of marsh,
metallic wings that never tire.
Dragon Queens' iron grip is harsh,
rescued eggs came from the fire.

Hovers over lake or river,
child-like monster nymphs emergent.
Hawker, Chaser, Darker quiver,
another ambush convergent.

Iridescent body seems to glow,
sunset changes yellow to gold.
Transparent wings dip and slow,
victory belongs to the bold.

Twenty-four thousand eyes alert,
darting flycatchers' witching hour.
Khalessi's bright appearance asserts,
armoured dragons' ancient power.

They watch the Damsels in distress,
fluttered flight ensures swifts appear.
Dragon rejects the knight's caress,
acrobatic flight away from fear.

As reeds flourish in the lake-side loam,
dragonflies haunt their wetland home.

THE KISSED PRINCE

Water-filled ditches of lost childhood,
from marsh to land, seemed at home.
Gone from where the Heron stood,
under any stone, you've known.

What gene pool did your spawn,
spring into jelly helix of life?
Pool and ponds face another dawn,
dodging the cruel schoolboy's knife.

Croak your love, extol hope forlorn,
she may be waiting to hear your plea.
Return alone; where bred and born,
heart and soul will soon be free.

Princess breeze kissing skin,
left her spluttered false caress.
She'll not dare to love you less,
if you produce her kith and kin.

Mysterious ripples stir elfin ponds,
quivering blanket of reedy fronds.
Silken lily pads rock to and fro,
as giants root beneath the flow.

Others moving, invisible, alive,
hewn heron stands statue still.
One false move and on his bill,
use silt camouflage to survive.

Eyes above surface
Spreading spawn string of pearls
Jam jars, nets; await

EIGHT-LEGGED SEAMSTRESS

Dew suspends, from gossamer steel,
wafted in dawn's cooling breeze.
As tremulous sails without a keel,
surprising beauty lightly breathes,

Tiny gnats' black wings unfurled,
joined by others in joyous flight.
Soon, an innocent of this world,
the sweet deceit of scuttling fright.

No rescue; invisible lair,
wind carries the desperate plea.
Now struggles in a sticky fear,
trapped in a cage of destiny.

Here she comes, wires a-humming,
her lisped whisper quiets all fear.
Soothing, gentle full of cunning,
'Come, accept your fate, my dear.

There's no escape, my sweet thing,
Stop your struggles, there is no gain'
Diaphanous death free of sin,
'a little bite will ease the pain'.

She weaves in gathered gloom,
views her sewing, oh, so proud.
Venomous tailor without a loom,
her victim's silken funeral shroud.

Now her children run down for tea,
a stitch in time means no escape.
Luscious bluebottle and tiny flea,
their mother's web took time to make.

CHECK MATE

'Hey, purple tongued freak, who are you?
Neck so long, hardly touch your toes.
Little horns, no good for rutting,
how do you even keep your footing?'

'Didn't they have the paint to finish,
looks so streaky, from down here'.
Giggling laughter from the troop,
as baboon chief moves too near.

Giselle, replied, between her munching
'My neck is long to reach the leaves,
my lovely tongue brings food to me,
never have to climb a tree'.

'Touch my toes? I'm super fit,
my horns just fine for butting foes.
My streaky skin is just fine,
a chess board slightly out of line'.

'Don't have to flee or fight,
my paint job keeps me out of sight.
Don't have to run scared and squealing
when the leopard comes death-dealing'.

'So, monkey-boy, I'm not a freak,
if I had thumbs, I'd rule the world.
Mr Baboon what's your story,
why've you missed that train to glory?'

BROOKIE

Silver wraith steadies, feels the power,
survival; is this his final hour.
Unquestioning soldier, his duty done,
bravely faced the current head on.

Faded light still kissed his realm,
with no lost sailor at the helm.
Nymph, desperate for life anew,
slowly rises, a damsel blue.

A sudden swirling quiet swish,
beautiful damsel becomes a dish.
Prince of the brook glides around,
retakes his place in the feeding ground.

Rosetta gems, gold flank alight,
a flick of the tail, gone from sight.
Hidden within his brook pristine,
implausible beauty rarely seen.

But beware, the faltering light,
a stutter, a twist it's not quite right?
Give this little nymph a miss,
whetted hook; your lasting kiss.

Angler will never know the cause,

saw a rise, not the nervous pause.

Old heron sends him on his way,

he'll catch Brookie another day.

Wearily home, light heart, empty creel,

teased by his children for their lost meal.

BEAUTY IN THE BLUEBELLS

Brave clouds chase stars from their cradle,
lost in a startled moment unknown.
Warm air filled with floating angels,
after dandelions' children have flown.

My sister tense enough to warn,
puffball angel perched on her nose.
Giggle stifled, her curled lip scorns,
I side-step and take to my toes.

Her tawney coat and shining eyes,
black lined ears and whiskers quiver.
Should the same silhouette arise,
when I drink in nearby river?

Off again, I'm teased to follow,
dainty tiptoe in bluebell clouds.
Hidden in a pine tree hollow,
black ballet shoes, brush pollen shrouds.

Light plays on painted ladies' dance,
fluttered burlesque feigns submission.
Patient beaus await their chance,
hope: fair maid will grant permission.

Far off we hear the tolling bells,

pull sturdy worms forward and back.

Tug-of-war joy between the knells,

winner takes all, a juicy snack.

Our earth beckons, mum's shrilling cry,

all danger lurks, in lost twilight.

Melted shadows refuse to lie,

not brave enough to stand and fight.

We curl upon dark earthen floor,

start to doze in familiar warmth.

See Sis's nose peek through her paws,

sweet dreams; her brush flicks back and forth.

RUB OF THE GREEN

Milling to and fro on some sacred green,
Champion bowlers will be crowned this day.
Horse-tail clouds are high and rink grass pristine,
tea-urns stoked, sandwiches, cakes on display.

Each teams' match-day colours wore a crown,
Woodland team resplendent in Sherwood green.
The Farmyard crew bedecked in russet brown,
even the crowd maintained the wildlife theme.

The teams were a mixture of old and new,
owl, fox, heron, hare – a wily bunch.
Not as well-mannered as the other crew,
sheepdog, rooster, pig and Suffolk punch.

Last years' Champions - on the mat by right,
combatants wave as they enter the rink.
Owl's heroes stretch and warm-up for the fight,
skip Tawney holds the jack, takes time to think.

She bowls the jack with sedate precision,
using silent signals, no rules to bend.
Yellow jack centred by joint decision,
all set as they commence the first end.

Claws on mat, Tawny lines up with great care,
first bowl away so smooth with her light tread.
Disaster, her glasses left on the chair,
she had let go a sleeping mole instead.

Rapt crowd, held their collected breath as one,
the un-biased mole rolled straight and true.
Waking up, blinking, almost halfway there,
she stopped, blushed, bowed and quietly withdrew.

Dozing Scarecrow ref now took centre stage,
decides Tawney could replay her bowl.
The crowd are now totally engaged,
some fun booing, even Hen shouts 'foul'.

All the players fought, and showed their worth,
heron struggled to get her knees down low.
Fox debonair, Scottie's hooves scuffed the turf,
Shep chasing players bowls, until her go.

In dimming light, spotlight on Harry hare,
squint-eyed he took deliberate aim.
But unnerved by Fox's sly, lascivious stare,
delivered the final bowl just the same.

Unfortunately, misreading the bias,
his bowl rolling in the wrong direction.

Near flattened a family of field mice,
shunting Pig's bowl to win, by deflection.

Winners met with sedate, polite applause,
as most victory or defeat dictates.
All on the victors' podium of course.
because it's tea and Kipling's best cakes.

BABY'S RATTLE

Dry vast desert winds are quieted too soon,
coarse slithering, head flat on sandy dune.
Cock crowed thrice, beckons new pretender,
appears a Basilisk from another era.

Lidless eyes, clarions a wary pause,
defence; a mirror to a martyr's cause.
Those eyes flat, a baleful abyss of hate,
you can turn your head, alas too late.

Venom dripping on the fertile ground,
was this land haven, in any circumstance?
Or perhaps too late, the Gods also found,
poison seeping from their shield and lance.

Coyote, wolf, human, hear and take care,
demonic rattle heard above their cries.
Paralysed prey, skewered can't take fright,
one look, her opaque eyes kill on sight.

Creeping heat soothes the cold within,
was she changing before our eyes?
Shed her legend and her skin,
schizophrenic sisters scorn the lies.

Nostrils flare; deadly musk caught on breeze,
if sly mongoose or weasel stalk; beware.
Alas too late to slither, or to freeze,
can't lead that slim destroyer to her lair.

Cruel swift bite behind the regal crest,
now, limp and lifeless without a battle.
The brindled killer purveys the nest,
drawn deep inside by the baby's rattle.

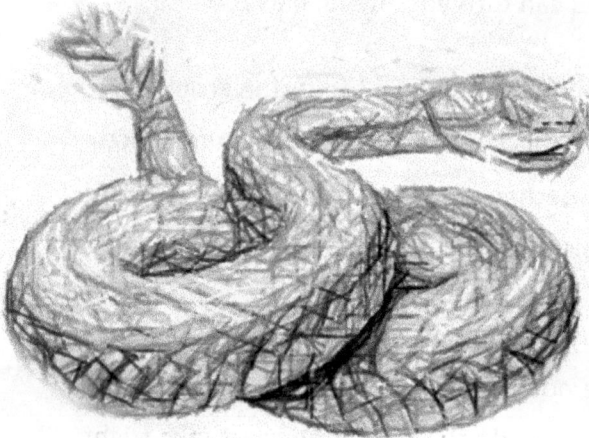

DESCEND TO PURGATORY

Another day, another show,
hear crowd's anticipation plea.
Agitated; swim to and fro,
wondering what they see in me.

Another day, another show,
know I'm dying, of this I'm sure.
Island cage of piteous sorrow,
Papillon, how did you endure?

Another day, another show,
Orca sings blue ocean song.
Only in dreams, my soul will go,
to paradise where I belong.

Another day, another show,
a seal-skinned mistress makes me tick.
Drenched front row penguins want to know,
how I perform my hardest trick?

Another day, another show,
descending beyond morbid black.
With captive heart immersed in woe,
losing, hopeless can't make it back.

Another show, another day,
now see the seals on land instead.
Screaming penguins on ocean's tow,
her skin in my teeth, bathed in red.

STRIPES EARNT

Stoic, sturdy, stubborn beasts of burden,
not seen for the beauty of their heart.
Broad of back, rough; no silken touch for them,
nor golden carriage, a farmer's cart.

But hark? Sound of joyful children's laughter,
ice creams, donkey rides for those who're good.
All day in the sun, no straw-filled rafter,
cloudy eyes, dry muzzle, only a hood.

Dreams of Zebra herds running wild and free,
yearns to don that stripey coat.
But poor Jack, it was never meant to be,
another day, another pack to tote.

Clovelly smugglers row into quiet quay,
hear flint-stone cobbles sing as they pass.
Stolen loot from poor wretches drowned at sea,
left abandoned without their braying ass.

Carried their saviour to his birth and death,
ever gentle, for precious cargo borne.
Any stumble, hallowed angels left bereft,
cross's shadow forever marked a coat, so torn.

Last cudgel struck; boot, fist and curse stayed,
Jack and Jenny; lift up your noble mane.
You'll join those carefree herds – debt repaid,
rewarded in your master's new domain.

GENTLE GIANT

Rain mist lifts off breathing mountain green,
as if in some animated story.
Verdant filtered light murmured glory,
grey mountains forested soulful scene.

Silver-backed Giant creased brow unfurled,
disciplined boss but caring, gentler dad.
Seen angry - posturing but never bad,
poachers and loggers have re-shaped his world.

They are not fooled by the look on his face,
as he now scans his family troop.
Safety first, the careful nannies scoop,
naughty babies and toddlers just in case.

Relentlessly logged, hunted, dwindling home,
when the forests are gone, where will he roam?

A Songbird's Lament

A Songbird's Lament

Interestingly, the title of this remarkable and original collection has two wholly plausible meanings: due to the unending despoliation of the countryside the songbirds' species are under threat together with their tuneful voice, hence their lament - and we in turn rue the absence of their music.

However, the sombre mood is relieved by sharp insights into avian behaviour, given vibrancy by a combination of strong emotional feelings and fresh imagery. The reader is therefore not just saddened but also educated and entertained. The playful wren '...flits in and out of the stone wall...' ever mindful of her feeding duties '...nestlings weeping for their fill...'.

What becomes clear is the poet's deep appreciation of the countryside coupled with anger at man's relentless urge to exploit Mother Nature's riches '...weed has grown, the bank recedes...' and '...farms push further, wetlands clearing...' a hint of danger too from '...glutinous silt...'. Also, he wonders if the curlew's cry in the vanishing fens echoes Mother Nature's tears.

Human imagery is used throughout with great success: the clutch of black crows in the shopping precinct resembling a '...gang intent on mischief...' the strutting march of the jackdaws '...in single file...'.

The kingfisher makes a welcome appearance '...this flash of iridescent steel...' which provokes a moment of wry humour as we are presented with '...the fishless angler's envious stare...' as the bird secures its latest catch! As in the title, musical imagery is cleverly employed '...the blackbird's aria...' and '...the choral song swirling with buzzing air...' - similarly there is the almost operatic impact of the '...murmuration symphony...'.

There is also modernity to emphasize natural beauty - a breathtaking image of geese in flight '...vies Red Arrows' sky display...'.

These inspired and moving verses provide a timely reminder of what we have lost together with a warning of what we may yet lose in the future.

Terry Carter

MASK OF RED AND GOLD

their natural habitat is built upon
    no verdant leafy glade, still singing strong
adapting to the gardener's glory
    chicks chirrup of a different story

yellow and burnished scarlet bird will feed
    on sad Vincent's yellowed sunflower seed.
a breed born prouder than the common finch
    takes a sudden flight at the slightest flinch

She lets the marching magpie pose and strut
    leaving the un-wanted suet ball and nut
Goldie flitting in and settling fast
    will thresh the seed as if the last.

the proud goldfinch will never fly to arm
    they group together as one golden charm
never deign to sing for some stolen crust
    nor to lose their dignity, in a swirl of dust

WHAT'S GOOD FOR THE GOOSE

Goose is the soldier

Hissing, strident, preening stance,
sentinel steadfast as the Tower chimes.
Feathered guard dog of Roman times,
better a honk than a guardian lance.

Goose is the sailor

Migrating geese oceanic flock,
with feeding grounds far from home.
Above all seas of froth and foam,
their mental compass finds dry dock.

Goose is the pilot

Better flyers are hard to find,
this flying team in fine array.
Vies Red Arrows in sky display,
and never leave a friend behind

Goose is cooked

Supermarket pate, French sue for slander.
Goose for Scrooge – that Christmas fable,
hungry youngsters round the table.
What's good for goose is good for gander

DARK BEAUTY

I stand astride a ladder stile,
as twilight steals the day.
Mischievous leaves dance awhile,
in chaotic disarray.
Giant oaks form witches' claws,
crows roost their crooked fingers.
Oak wilt weeps like open sores,
as cloying damp still lingers.

Our world prepares for icy cold,
curls up and cowers down.
Ancient tree roots soon unfold,
accepting winter's frown.
Softer tread makes no mistake,
dark silence drapes anew.
Coax nocturnal life to wake,
as light turns deeper blue.

Sad lonely screech plays its part,
how spiritually she calls.
Signal for the night to start.
as Astraea's veil must fall.
She calls again, beguiles the tree,
a challenge to intrude.
Daylight shadows haste to flee,
dark beauty's solitude.

THE MESSENGER

Crows; smartest kid on the block,
forms a murder not a flock.
Looks like a cruel gang intent,
on mischief, and dark accident.

Through the ages stridently warn,
of possible tragedies and waifs forlorn.
A symbol then devilishly meant,
these harbingers of historical event.

Oh, Guardian cobalt blue and black,
quietly watching from the back.
Malice seeping from every pore,
stealthy sentries at devil's door.

Calling, caw such sad lament,
Vikings hear the message sent.
Mysterious runic tales to tell,
of souls Valhalla bound, not hell.

Coronis, Apollo's mistress fair,
left her God for simpler fayre.
In vengeful wrath he turned his back,
named her crow! burnt her black.

Zombies, witches? there're just for show,
nothing so chilling as a crow.
Halloween wouldn't be the same,
their dark shadow stalks every game.

Out of town shopping mall,
a seagull could never be a pal.
As guardians hunched in every tree,
they patrol the bins at KFC.

A pair will swoop down on a kite,
fearless warrior in a fight.
If one should die, for comrades' sake,
they join their neighbours in a wake.

Throughout the ages always mean,
tormenting Hawks a grisly scene.
In the background killing time,
crows will never walk the line.

SWEET JENNY WREN

Jenny wren trills an early morn,
in and out of that dry-stone wall.
That sombre early daylight torn,
does another beau hear your call?

Pulls aside dew-stained ivy vine,
displaces morbid insect strife.
Watches, darting, stoops to dine,
secures hope for another's life.

Gardener leans on tired fork,
expose larvae to razor bill
Wren, nimble, tireless mother's work,
nestlings weeping for their fill.

Thin-beaked, tail erect so proud,
so small the songbird; yet so loud.

WHO WILL CHORUS THE DAWN?

When another songbird dies,
what deafening silence met.
Blackbird warbles in chilled surprise,
will children care to listen yet?

Chaffinch, chiff-chaff, hoped for echo,
robin never short of silence.
Lost; Curlew's warbled crescendo,
nightjar hammering makes no sense.

Where is that dawn chorus for my child?
Must the songbirds sing their last good-bye?
Forever lost the joy of the wild,
who will rejoice their last descant cry?

Think, think back in time, not so long,
no river sewers, just new birth.
Lark and thrush burst with life and song,
listened then, paradise on earth.

Now, silence is the only sound,
no time to sing, no time to breathe.
Hear Ocean's Sirens all around,
is this the planet you bequeath?

Unbalanced faltering towards the brink,

what was that? A birdsong?

No, a tipping point, I think.

DRONE KILLER

She was torn from bleak twilight,
silver white, russets dimmed.
Corpse-silent when in flight,
too innocent to have sinned.

Austere moon a turreted lantern,
bathed the scene; spectre – shiver.
Her feathers daubed at every turn,
even graced Apollo's quiver.

Ethereal mists weave the pines,
never shrouding her hooded eyes.
Quartered back a hundred times,
old wise patience sieving lies.

There - a sudden blur of white,
soundless sadness met with silence.
Once white in majestic flight,
now lifeless, his soul gone hence.

Her once sweet prince, just blood and bone,
her dissolving heart an empty husk.
With their owlets' fate unknown,
no more joyful hunt at dusk.

At first light a boys' heart raced,
his father's promise, tonight's the night.
Their walk in the forest to be faced,
his birthday drones' inaugural flight.

Hovers at first with laboured moves,
then braver swoops and sharper turns.
Fading light, mum disapproves,
allowed, one last late meteor burn.

Never saw the mystical flight,
novice eyes, control and feel.
The sickening crash gave him a fright,
once white - now scarlet - a fox's meal.

Mottled grief drowned in blood,
forest hidden echoes absorb the pain.
But even in the darkest wood,
a shaft of light enshrines hope – again.

An owlet totters, almost fledged,
mother, exhorting daughters' flight.
Swoops down from the nest edge,
lightest feathers kiss the night.

Mottled Sorcerer

Estuary bleak in the watery sun,
harsh-edged reeds and teasel blown.
Two are wading, without a gun,
both at peace, the world's their own.

Weaved through the shivering reeds,
a ghostly cry, a woman's scream.
I glanced at my father, did he heed?
Thought I still slept in my dreams.

'That's a Curlew boy, they're very rare,'
that curdling cry rose yet again.
I sensed a haunting in the air,
it sounded like a babe in pain.

Not for me the snipe or whimbrel,
my curlew surely evokes the clatter,
of the courtiers' Parisian tumbril.
Wagtails copy the watcher's chatter.

We trap birds for no personal gain,
to find safe haven in Hope Farm.
That evocative bubbling call again,
stood frozen still, hand on arm.

Reeds parted, a pale shaft of sun,
scimitar beak, looking harsh.
Strange, stooped wading step never run,
Mottled Sorcerer of the marsh.

Farms expand, wetlands clearing,
marshes, peat bogs disappearing.
Now, no more Curlew call to hear,
her demise echoes Natures' tears.

THE OLD MAN OF THE RIVER

Watched for nettles, as I slowed my pace,
glimpsed the river swathed in sighs.
Breathed, as early morning fingers trace,
red streaks across awakened skies.

Stepped light over weeded mound,
spied a moorhen with her brood.
Dragonfly's glassy brittle sound,
assuaging any bitter mood.

Whispering reedbeds in the breeze,
fondly caress lily pads below.
Felt myself begin to ease,
watch grey plover's ariel show.

Stopped; looked somewhat in dismay,
there standing in the shallows.
A hunched old man in grey,
turbulence, eddy, eye that follows.

Thinking he might need some aid,
gently called to him out loud.
Turned to me with a smile that played,
as sunlight peeks through a cloud.

Strange yellow eyes in spectacles,
wispy black hair down his back.
Stooped past the darting damsels,
he kept my pace along the bank.

'I'm Hragra, come for a proper look,
weed has grown; the bank recedes.
When I was young, I must concede,
t'was a lovely babbling brook'.

A halting strange deliberate gait,
he waded slowly near the bank.
His steely eyes beheld his fate,
glutinous silt, but he never sank.

'My children have cried to me,
water is no longer crystal clear.
Oh, Hragra the fish will all soon flee'.
As he turned, I saw a tear.

Leaving, thought my heart might rend,
hesitated, looked back to see.
A heron – by the river bend,
where Hragra first appeared to me.

THE KING AND I

Twisting like a braided rope,
crystal river can never lie.
A glint, a glimpse, a hope,
of sweet surrender in a lover's eye.

Giggles, gurgles as sunlight skips,
meanders; drunken party zeal,
A kingfisher's flight lightly dips,
a flash of iridescent steel.

Proud King of Fishers keenest eye,
halcyon of the river's health.
Dart of orange, more zip than fly,
speed of arrow cloaked in stealth.

No shadow drives the fry's reaction,
flits from willowherb to reed.
Head turned, challenges refraction,
warrior's dagger remains unsheathed.

Water cleaved, a hooded feat,
fluttered, ignited feather flare.
Minnow held, her dark eyes meet,
fishless angler's envious stare.

Molten metal blue

Icarus bird of the sun

Plumage you have won

OH, TO FLY

Shaken softly awake, my prince, arise!
Now together, we have far, far to fly.
Hear that lone beseeching call from on high,
bravely soaring towards a new sunrise.

Russet feathers arch through thermal waves,
winged fingers stretch an octave at least.
Spurs his bold heart for the speed he craves,
not till then, will he rip his first feast.

Midnight blue sapphires patterned dunes,
faceted jewel absorbs careless hate.
Often, reflects self-inflicted wounds,
shapeshifting desert sealed his fate.

Lost eyes - a myriad of dancing play,
kaleidoscope of a multi-coloured maze.
Abandoned mountains left far away,
searching; his torn soul for what he craves.

Twist in time recalls his first love,
still feels tortured pain, deep inside.
Surely his wounded soul could rise above,
her cold heart and his sin of pride.

In his confusion, yet unsure,
another offers unfolded wing.
Wrapped within them now feels secure,
a chance at last, for him to sing?

SONG OF FORGIVENESS

Love beats in a bright red breast,
perched high in your heavy heart.
Melodic plea from his nest,
trills hopeful for our fresh start.

Smile; as I hear this sweet sound,
despite harsh snow on the ground.
His sharp tune sears through the white,
comforts us throughout the night.

Missiles deluged like hard rain,
we weathered the storm, so dire.
Earth, betrayed, chose ice not fire,
we need hope to start again.

What chorus tomorrow may bring,
never needs us there to thrive?
Bravest note his soul will sing,
though few, so glad we survived.

To sing sweet forgiveness is divine,
although freely given - did I earn mine?

MURMURATION SYMPHONY

Choral choir of sweet togetherness,
swirled in the buoyancy of the air,
Swoop; shapeshifters in perfect harness,
hear heart and wing beat harmonies shared.

They're joined by another, then still more,
phalanx of warriors without a war.
Hear a thousand wing tips click-click, click-click,
soaring symphony to a conductor's flick.

Rising in tumultuous accord,
an aria seared chord by chord.
Concert tenor in ecstasy fervour,
lost in the intensity of his ardour.

Suddenly gone, now silent; cold,
hush; hear the first crocus unfold.
Silken rain falls in rainbowed pools,
blue night around us softly cools.

MELODIC HEART

Fledgling blackbird's pure aria all aglow,
eager juvenile thrusts for offered worms.
Lungs so tiny, in beating breast must grow,
but just listen; we'll hear that song confirmed

Statues; those sacred trees in silence rapt,
listen intently for that melodic score.
Oh, marvel at that sound but never trapped,
bellows from deep within his tiny core.

His breast will rise and fall with that refrain,
his repleted heart never has to strive.
Cossetted in a spiritual terrain,
telling us all - he's glad to be alive.

What does his song mean to the waiting world?
Learnt from instinct cocooned within his nest.
Revels in those first sweet notes unfurled,
sadly, the song is not at our behest.

Tells us a tale of his nation's story,
joyous, despite the loss and grief embalmed.
Triumph note echoes nature's glory,
now peaceful, as his troubled soul is calmed.

DISTANT COUSINS

Light is lost as grey shrouded jackdaws walk,
sedate as monks to their vesper trance.
Quieted now, not for them a wayward squawk,
heads bowed to their hallowed vow of silence.

Walk, in single file on ancient coping,
it seems the raucous starling flight ignored.
Simply aware of the sun that's setting,
their silhouettes still don't look untoward.

Easier to confuse their darker looks,
not irreverent cawing of the rooks.
Darkly, black as coal with a hint of blue
but their grey hoods in conspicuous hue.

Although Corvus traits to see,
neglected to roost on the family tree.

HEAVEN'S BIRDHOUSE

Chaffinch, Wren and Siskin,
flutter on the bird feeder.
They know what they're risking,
but their chicks are needier.

Watched by noisy neighbours,
envious of their pluck.
Let others copy their labours,
take a chance on potluck.

Hung off the birdhouse floor,
every breed braver still.
Unafraid; we were sure,
as our friends took their fill.

When true fear is absent.
heartening thought for us all,
Angels' feathers heaven sent,
as we hear nature's call.

RENEWAL

The nightingale one of most endangered yet most beautiful songsters. The blackbird has a sweet note but only has two phrases, the nightingale has a thousand. Thought, in times gone by, to sing of love, hope and renewal.

He treads softly in a darkened glade,
the silence soothes his soul.
Heartfelt sorrows of tangled grief,
time heals; but takes its toll,
His damaged heart is unafraid.
he shuns that false relief.

His tranquillity is soon pierced,
by a song on stolen air.
Spoke to that lost inner boy,
who'd forgotten how to care.
Like his first damned hit of morphine,
mixed ecstasy and joy.

Moonlight, not grey or silver hue,
but somewhere in-between.
Russet brown caught in a beam,
not scarlet, gold or blue.
Madam nightingale deigned to preen,
brief beauty rarely seen.

71

Seductive siren, secret satyr,
notes a little crisper.
She sees inside his numbing pain.
when her song's a whisper.
Perhaps enticed by that sweet refrain,
the wind wants him to hear.

A thousand songs, her repertoire,
as her symphony floats,
healing those swaying trees,
with sad melancholic notes,
Her pure heart swells with love and more,
to haunt the sullen breeze.

Notes filled with melody and ache,
language that lovers seek.
Hidden passions calm the beast,
allow his heart to speak.
What feelings wash away his guilt,
his tears, a soul's release.

A future singing to his past,
embalms a brand-new start,
White shawl and baby shoes not worn,
tiny casket in his heart.
Perhaps he'll find some peace at last,
a chance to be reborn.

Passion for the Environment

Passion for the Environment

The author's insights into the natural world and its human connections were very much in evidence in his first anthology. However, *Tears of the Wolf Moon* introduced us to more connected consciousness of the environment and its precious existence and vulnerability.

He has drawn on a lifetime's experience of rivers, wildlife (especially ornithology) and his particular strong suit, angling – as in **Summer Love** *'Swooping swifts dimple its opaque fortitude, absent breeze leaves cool surface undisturbed'*.

The work shows an unwavering awareness of our responsibilities as a human race. Both towards the natural world and threats from countless directions, often vainly justified and disguised as 'progress'. Nowhere is this sentiment portrayed than in the poem

Noah's Warning – 'Those floodgates open Devil's bowl, drowning cries of sweet nature's soul'.

His profound experience of many current environmental issues has been delivered in a poetic style and freshness of approach which is born of a genuine affinity which transcends any political agenda. He has been fortunate to be able to sample the local delights of his North Buckinghamshire home countryside as well as many a trout stream... along with a plethora of babbling Scottish brooks.

David Carrington

AUTUMNAL RETREAT

Children splash puddled paths,
squirrels chased through autumn leaves.
Mum reprimands, dad just laughs.
Giggles; as in and out they weave.

Wellies abandoned in the yard,
roaring fire, hot chocolate ready.
Kids toast marshmallows, dad on guard,
mums on brandy, wee bit heady.

Children tired and it's off to bed,
can't wait up for the Harvest Moon.
All teary sleep-tights have been said,
autumnal darkness comes too soon.

Dying sun plays tricks of light,
flickers on a child's rested face.
Dust motes reflect welcome night,
day disappears and leaves no trace.

Misty, cloying autumnal scent,
every leaf-shaped amethyst.
Decayed, fungi thrusts assent,
moss creeps into rock and crevice.

Time seeps slow as rusty clocks,
hedgehog drifting golden slumbers.
Skies filled with migrating flocks,
fallen leaves for once outnumbered.

Ghostly orange haloes light,
Victorian gaslight of the dusk.
Noise slithers but stays out of sight,
mist camouflages vixens' musk.

Old bookshop aroma pervades,
skeletal boughs, nests suspended.
Now crows roost the dripping shade,
await another autumn ended.

Spring Morning by the Lake

Warming mist fingers will silently trace,
as new sunlight enshrines the placid scene.
Reflects soft lights of chestnut, oak and space,
a magical world of what might have been.

Ancient Oak's bony fingers reach for light,
statuesque sculptures, cast in serenity.
A sturdier perch for a watchful Kite,
surrounds us in deliberate beauty.

Sit silently; let Nature come to you,
quieter then, breathe deep to bare your soul.
She speaks so softly in the morning dew,
somehow, the frantic world still takes its toll.

Bankside reeds, surround gnarled long-lived ash,
seems to shelter another world below.
Mallards hold court with preening rise and splash,
as newborn sun makes the lakeside glow.

Hawthorne blossom reminds of forgotten snow,
splash of gold as daffodils swell in bloom.
Soft breeze coax willow trees to sway, so slow,
as life emerges from Winter's gloom.

Thrush and robin spy angler's squirming bait,
taunt him; hope to avert his focused eyes.
But he just smiles and patiently awaits,
treasured moments even without a prize.

New symphony from above to below,
songbirds loudly chorus the season change.
As morning listens for lone soprano,
harmony pitch perfect in blackbird's range.

Surely swap proud swan, for soiled city sprawl,
hear wood pigeon sit, cooing with his dove.
Spent all my life hearing this wildlife call,
knowing I was meant for nature's love.

Distant church bell tolls an hourly chime,
the only evidence of man's lost time.
Rings for peace into this awakened world
life bursts replete, into hearts unfurled.

HUMANS ARE GONE

Humans are gone
who will miss them?

Spring awakes
Summer blooms
Autumn falls
Winter shivers

Animals re-appear
Fish now swim near
Insects won't sting
Birds can sing

Rivers flow clean
Sea tides preen
Sky ozone heals
Wild land, no fields

Happily, mountains pierce clouded fury,
their snowbound laughter echo peaks revealed.
Who will miss man from this repleted world,
as just another distant memory?

THE AVENUE

Those brooding darkened black hills mock,
the rising, slate volcanoes slain.
Water swirls allow depths unlock,
soothes angry Titan's final pain.

Will-o-wisp mist, seems to hang,
spiral, towering pines afar.
Fir cone bouncing unheard by man,
and tumbles to the forest floor.

Moves beneath night's breathless dew,
sentinel toadstools strive to see.
Continued death gives life anew,
fungi push through aged debris.

Light into dark, the beaver's nurse,
other creatures to see the day.
Invertebrate thriving universe,
dark; inviting forever grey.

Through avenues of arching bows,
soft-focus emerald altars.
Lovers will soon be making vows,
unquenched love that never falters.

Secret view as paradise nears,
sepia tones in slow-fading light.
Hidden lake mysteries appear,
surface blemished by martin's flight.

Stray light caught; spiders' silk reflects,
zephyr breeze beauty now unfurled.
Diaphanous gem moon effects,
and lilies wear a string of pearls.

WILDERNESS SONG

Awake; the startled plains betrayed,
stained in brooding loss and blood.
Desolate songs bled through the grass,
from tribes extinct no debt repaid.
Beseeched to save but no one could,
screams torn from tears of distant past.

Bonfire sparks light up the gloom,
sage scent incense pervades their soul.
Nostalgic dreams of the unknown,
enchants the desert to dance and bloom.
Voiced tributes raise to extoll,
spirals up to their holy home.

Stamped moccasin brings grief to life,
an ancient Apache chanted song,
Howl their pain on the faded sun,
opioid cry for nature's strife.
Exhort ancients to right the wrong,
laments the cruel torment to come.

Their wilderness of joy now abandoned,
their lands are gone, nobility stripped.
Casinos replace brittlebush flowers,

for the whirr of the wheel that thundered.
Slot halls, bingo and poker chip,
swapped their teepee for the towers.

Wilderness swathed in Paloverde bloom,
not desolate desert, scrub, and scree.
Shows us a beauty of our dreams,
where every creature sings in tune.
The wilderness is not wild, but free,
hidden in plain sight, it seems.

NATURE-LOVING VOLUNTEER

Nature depleting; rapid rate,

some won't sit, watch it dissipate.

They are striving to quell our fears,

those selfless nature Volunteers

Volunteer strides river and dell,

Water Boards their filth expel.

Never stopping at dying fish,

now scared what's on the Petrie dish.

Stem those paving over beauty,

ceaseless river walking duty.

They stand tall, fulfil their role,

what they see takes a toll.

To introduce the beaver,

never see the plants and sedge.

To build an oaken bird box,

never see the owl chicks fledge.

To dredge a silted, dying stream,

never see flash flood recede.

To build a draughty watcher's hide,

nor see shy curlew parting reed.

To plant a spreading chestnut tree,
never to sit in soothing shade.
Building banks to save a river,
never see it bend and braid.

Clearing river's invasive weed,
never to see the path it's made.
To eradicate mink and cray,
never see a vole on parade.

Yet plucky volunteers still strive,
to keep beloved nature alive.
To save a whale or plant a tree,
for everyone's grandchild to see.

Noah's Warning

Rising, rising, watery hell,
breaks banks in remorseful fury.
Watching the river gorge and swell,
neighbour's abandoned misery.

Denied Beaver's miraculous craft,
blocked river's meandering course.
Visible sludge smeared aftermath,
lone man can't beat the water's force.

Scared morning awakened so silently,
black skies signal impending doom.
Paying river's last penalty,
for badly built defenceless homes.

Repeated entreaties unheard,
can't clean gullies, ditches and drains.
All answers sounding quite absurd,
developers mouth sour refrain.

Our heroine in mortal garb,
Flood Mary hears the clarion call.
Advising, helping homes to guard,
assuage her pain for one and all.

River listens; then flowing on,

awaits cruel rain to gorge again.

Not a sprint, but a marathon,

once again to release the pain.

Those floodgates open Devil's bowl,

drowning cries of sweet nature's soul.

THE LIVING RIVER

I am river; forever born,
waters broken awakened glow.
Brutally from the soil I'm torn,
ripped from nurturing womb below.

Pushes, thrusting through the earth,
gurgled, bubbles, flowing outwards.
Mother Rain's umbilical birth,
continue my path, ever forwards.

Brothers, cousins, sisters unite,
we; becoming more than one.
Journey to our ancestor's light,
destiny demanded our sweet song.

Mewled, dependent, am I growing,
sleepless; reflects distant starlight.
Skipped, splashes, joyous tumbling,
felt the meadow's verdant light.

Father sunlight, renew my life,
please, let me breathe the air you bring.
Sensed small creatures you saved from strife,
alive! see them dance, see them sing.

My new force cuts a pathway through,
rockface resistant as a child.
I must go on towards the blue,
no granite barriers beguiled.

Gouges, forcing any weakness,
rock that softens is worn down.
If too strong for my caress,
I will turn and go around.

Feel that freedom as I flow,
power from a deeper bed.
Tickling gravel as I grow,
lost in wonder at the road ahead.

I am rapids, rock is steeper,
tumbling foam in whirlpool light.
Steadier, slow, swirls much deeper,
feel fish in fast current fight.

I am estuary, slow and wide,
Meanders, unsure, still on track?
Breathe the wonderous swell and tide,
once joined with sea, I will be back.

NATURE'S HEALING BALM

Aching soul; you cannot breathe,
loving river will help relieve.
Massage your body wracked with pain,
eddying currents heal again.

Awake: cruel night won't set you free,
escape in chorus symphony.
You wear that wounded thorny frown?
Watch sergeant Magpie play the clown.

When martyred beneath tumbrel wheels,
walk the meadow, sweet fragrance heals.
Deep dusted book you should've read,
wildflowers soothe what's in your head.

Hurt by the casual barbarous tongue,
playful fox cub will right that wrong.
A victim of your world's torment,
sense wood anemone's magical scent.

Cynical smiles tear hidden tears,
blackbird's song heals those tortured fears.
Mauled by Black Dog that cannot bite.
feel incensed breeze on balmy night.

Devil's gold fiddles' last eerie notes,
starlight reflects in his tawney motes.
Broken arrow strung; but failed to fly,
watch golden eagle swoop purple sky.

Keep out of your own way fast.
face your unknown curses' cast.
Adapt and bend sure not to break,
like twisted teasels by the lake.

Seize the world, you will thrive,
nature's balm keeps you alive.

Winter Beach

Surly desolate beach berates us,
unbroken, bent marram grass survives.
Gulls' windswept lone mournful chorus,
sad fragility of heartfelt cries.

Our lovers' footprints in wetted sand,
unvanquished by a persistent tide.
Walk silently, still hand in hand,
bound, close together, side by side.

With chaste harried clouds flown north,
lost lovers to the sky return.
Overnight wicked chill marched forth,
frost nipped cheeks, blinded eyes that burn.

Pale winter sunlight starts to thaw,
hoare frosts' tentacles icy grip.
Feel the crunch of the glassy floor,
even Roe Deer could make a slip.

Snow drift swept by buffering wind,
cuts deeply through our veil of tears.
Paltry sunlight shapes windward dunes,
accords faint hope to all our fears.

See the azure sky command,

to vast horizons raise your eyes.

Chastened view of joy's demand,

peers kindly through that thin disguise.

Oh, Winter on the beach we yearned,

scorched away our season's blues.

Driftwood gathered; all sorrows burned,

another earth spin paid our dues.

Hands clasped tight, our cold cheeks touch,

tender whispered warm entreaties.

No comfortable fireside couch,

gladly swapped for winter beaches.

SEE ANOTHER WINTER?

When a snowflake dies, silence met,
will our supposed betters hear our soft prayers.
When a thousand flakes fall, lest we forget,
or winter herald our muddy tears.

Boom, boom; listened for an echo,
perhaps not on this silent night.
Quiet on quiet, silent crescendo,
of crackled snow no fire in sight.

Chattering teeth, breath blown in hands,
do songbirds sing in eventide?
A sweet note soars above the wires,
a beautiful hymn rejoicing life.

Not in any tongue we knew,
but the music fills our souls.
We knew the melody through and through,
for those who listened, paradise extolled

Now, silence, the competing sound,
as a note rises from our ranks.
Two songbirds beseech our hearts,
a Soldiers way of giving thanks.

Even in this wintery waste,
love has found a welcome place.

When You Feel

When I touch the cold black void,
do you catch me when I fall?

When my heart cries out in pain,
do you answer, when I call?

When I see an eagle soar,
are you anchored to the ground?

When I hear the Blue Whale sing,
do you ever hear a sound?

When I play a song by Dylan,
do you hear but never listen?

When I write for you alone,
do you focus on what's missing?

When I set the Goshawk free,
do you want to use a hood?

When I rest on a wooden cross,
do you wash your hands in blood?

When I sing a Navaho song,
do you call them savage?

When I adore the Wilderness,
do you pave and ravage?

When I yearn to be free,
do you seethe with jealous rage?

When I sing a blackbird's song,
do you build a gilded cage?

When you see what I see,
are you blinded – just the same?

When you hear what I hear,
are you deafened by the shame?

When you feel what I feel,
then we'll truly be the same.

GODDESS OF SPRING

Spy the furze and gold broom reborn,
never the stunted leafy thorn.
Spring has woken reluctantly,
soon blind leveret's eyes will see.

Persephone decreed rebirth,
her subjects of flower and bark.
Sweet Goddess of Spring walks the earth,
released the bluebell from the dark.

Hear her bird's glorious chorus,
laying eggs speckled with secrets.
First brave soldier; purple crocus,
still missing them, less we forget.

Turns her head to the river hues,
coloured skies reflect her mood.
A different palette lights blue fuse,
rainbow colours of joy intrude.

This year's iced winter ground me down,
each sullen day oft wore a frown.
Awoken by her birds one dawn,
somehow, I almost felt reborn.

Senses alive heard buzzing bees,
snowdrops I hadn't seen before.
Hedgehog blinks from her reveries,
miasma scents from forest floor.

As watery sun fights the chill,
walk secret paths once closed to me.
Spot swallow nests by watermill,
nurse my coffee, I stroll to see.

Buds; giggling elves behind a door,
thrush and blackbird braver by far.
Serenade my walk with awe,
heartfelt song in my church's choir.

NOVEMBER'S CHILD

Her cunning, dirty urchin face,
will hardly raise a smile.
Scrawny, wild, can't hold her eye,
beware her rodent guile.
You're neither autumn, nor winter,
No; you're something in-between.

Scratches her face and pulls the threads,
eases Autumn's hold.
She guards her bowl of watery gruel,
to warm against the cold.
December's child scolds and cries,
don't splash her bridal gown.

Can't lift a hem and show a leg,
like sister March, so bold.
Gentlemen friends don't shower you,
in floral blue and gold.
Her prettiness makes you seethe,
she's never growing old.

Twelve siblings, some have sweeter names.
like April, May and June.
But they all have smiles to bring,
not squalls and suffering.
They cry remember, remember,
Wednesday's child; November.

KIND CURRENTS

Swirling pools of pewter moonlight,
black waters eddy to somewhere.
Cruel secrets hide impatient night,
kinder currents will heal the fear.

Water is life, life is water,
without it, we are all but dust.
Cuts tomorrow, asks no quarter,
if yesterday's sentence is just.

Ripples turn, meanders and cools,
weir gushes colour of old blood.
Tumbling ball of confusion pools,
back eddies swirl with weed and mud.

Ducks joyous, wagtails splash and bathe,
dipper clings on slimed moss stone.
Only otter dad cuts a swathe,
would never leave those pups alone.

This playground haven soon unveiled,
no Eden gardener would believe.
A child peeps as if sleep curtailed,
sun unravelled from slumbered eve.

River, hope you never change or slacken,
run swift through gorse and golden bracken.

Walk by the Church

A Churchyard wears a widow's shroud,
tolled bell peals, a hollow chime.
Each sad note stretched stolen time
gothic ravens form a crowd.

Crows play-fight near fated stones.
do sombre spirits hear their calls,
believe it's children tossing balls?
Peace and joy for those old crones.

Hands in pockets, a natty cap,
beats the early morning chill.
Short cut, has only time to kill,
simple track, doesn't need a map.

Senses unlock a life at peace,
he stops to listen, feels alone.
Soft silence strikes a mournful tone,
his spirit finds its own release.

Ravens, curious join the crows,
their rowdy noise soon fills the air.
Each telling tales with undue care,
who's in trouble? only heaven knows.

Careful tread between crooked stones,
wipes the webs and gathered moss.
Reads sad thoughts of time-faded loss,
what epitaph for his old bones?

A Season's Love

I was the river Lea,
she was my summer rain.
Softest choral refrain,
on my journey to the sea

I was the river Tees,
she was my dancer bright.
In the amber evening light,
shaded by the willow trees.

I was the river Tay,
she was my autumn gold.
Timeless secrets untold,
by evening light's dismay.

I was the river Usk,
she was my winter shawl.
Comforting my aging thrall,
shared my evening dusk,

I was the riverbed,
she was my spring revived.
Her rain kept me alive,
soundly slept; my torpor shed.

RETURN TO EDEN

Wildfires rage uncontested,
river's flooding, ice flows melt.
Cliffs erode and sorrow felt,
no hiding place, when tested.

Wildlife dies, species extinct,
habitat gone forever.
Man walks slowly to the brink,
perhaps it's now or never.

Plastic waste blocks our rivers,
poisoned oceans; hope unsalvaged?
Marine life shakes and quivers,
as their seabed's futures dredged.

As the world becomes tinder,
and the rivers have all run dry.
A burning, dry reminder,
that the world can't even cry.

Greta, what are you doing?
Will all your blah, blah, ferment?
Is it the world you're saving,
or just the human tenant?

Because when we are long gone,
the world will return to Eden.

Summer Love

Oh, to be cloaked in warming incensed air,
too soon we'll have to pay our summer's debts.
Quickly our absorbed, frantic mind forgets,
for once, we sleep and dream without care.

The drumming, drowsy, humming of the bees,
weaves a latticework of all our senses,
A light miasma of floral fragrances,
hypnotises the swaying chestnut trees.

As the sacred daylight does not encumber,
softer beauty seeks to embalm my soul.
Twilight dissolves prepared to play its role,
nocturnal life blinks awake from slumber.

Our path, though well-worn, was never lost,
as those before us, have remained eclipsed.
Sip nectar from a lover's fingertips,
in life's sweet tenderness embossed.

Portraying a stained-glass reflection, blurred,
the lakes' peace and restful solitude.
Swooping swifts dimple its opaque fortitude,
absent breeze leaves cool surface undisturbed.

Stall another season's relentless march,
and embrace again our summertime bliss?
It enchants and delights as a first kiss,
hold each other as we feel the world lurch.

TRANQUILLITY FOUND

A dragonfly tremulous in the breeze,
dronelike darts with glass wings chattering.
The warm air played with a river at ease,
settled, the reed bends, nods, still swaying.

Moorhens, back and forth, time is now short,
mum-to-be cajoling 'sticks, more sticks!'.
Even the Kingfisher seems lost in thought,
watching the lone stranger, quiet, transfixed.

Silently becoming one with Nature,
standing in the river, alone and tall.
Surrendering his very soul for cure,
releasing the chains of society's call.

His frantic feelings play hide and seek,
stops false idols that have pressed him down.
Tranquill river, listen; let her speak,
implores Danu to wear his crown.

The true innocence of Nature at peace,
silently allows his spirits release.

PLASTIC PALACE

Once swollen, turbulent, fluid, running free,
buoyed by silvery shimmered, surface light.
Penetrating once hidden depths of me,
but my darker psyche is kept from sight.

Watch the dolphins, sperm whales and Orcas play,
coral reef painted with rainbow colours.
Peace, solitude, day follows endless day,
wavelets pound soft drumbeats on sandy shores.

Felt a new magma modelling my soul,
glacial warming an unknown smoking gun?
Silver beaches black, as dumped plastics foul,
my volcanic paradise home undone.

Streams, rivers once found my ocean heart,
shoaled life evades my rudderless helm.
My womb an infant cradle for life's start,
mountains dare not encroach my darkest realm.

I'm now a slowed tidal current well spent,
alone now, lifeless flickering shadow.
Open veins that once coursed without relent,
now, sluggish, brackish, clogged and shallow.

My slowed heart beats as arteries grow hard,
currents, undertow and tides now wrench apart.
Bleaching my grief with thoughtless disregard,
oiled surface burns, stars turning inside out.

Can't watch as my terrified Orcas die,
infected mother's milk kills Blue Whales' calves.
Plastic squid are Logger turtle's new prey,
cruel nylon lines crossing Hammerhead paths.

Insane Sirens stand screaming in the shallows,
wail for their Tsunami God's vengeance.
Wreaked havoc in those deathly hallows,
who will write the world's final sentence?

Veins and arteries course once more,
nature insisting death before re-birth.
Stark bones now litter pebbled shore,
rise and fall on placated surf.

CLOUD WALKING

Knee-high river mist sleeps undisturbed,
ghostly roe deer too shy to dally.
Skeletal trees, old hag's fingers curved,
around moonlight, ill-advised to tarry.

Disowned tombstones form an inner cordon,
Citadel; phoenix of another time.
Knowing that forever is a burden,
reminds us, with every hallowed chime.

Crystal river, gypsy's silver ribbon,
braided ringlets, shades of my lover's hair.
Swirling, sad, dances to be forgiven,
leaving me lonely without a care.

Songbird chorus floods awakened hearts,
blackbird conducts A Capela style.
Trills glorious morning melody starts,
imploring skylarks, finches; 'Sing, a while'.

Cawing rooks try to lend more raucous skies,
ancient nests hanging basket, never neat.
Any riverbank approach, stills their cries,
Now watchful, their sentry works complete.

Rainbow, manoeuvre, hide in streamer weed,
tail flick, current mastered, caddis snatched.
Minnows, bullheads scatter, re-group and feed,
wild trout patient; await another hatch.

THE ANCIENTS

I have many rings, but not one to wed,
my black gnarled bark is worse than my bite.
I shed golden leaves for your bridal bed,
gentle breeze parts boughs to allow the light,

Ate my stolen fruit long before you sinned,
our fibrous roots – writing on the wall.
Bold branches sway, chattering in the wind,
sends messages when danger comes to call.

Sanctuary given to our nightingales,
our nurse Florence, without a bloodied gown.
Cleared sick bark of parasitic entrails,
squirrels ensure next generation grown.

We've lived history, seen it all before,
from lofty heights future visions unveil.
Our children survive through strife and war,
providing fossil fuels to no avail.

CIRCLE OF HOPE

A river remembers the old songs,
what does she sing today?
Her journey lasts a lifetime,
she has so much to say.
What tales she'll tell our children.
when they pause to listen.

Salmon know their own way home,
they leap in forgotten time.
Curlews call across the marsh,
Nature's renewal chime.
Otter prints seen once again,
dimple his old terrain.

Great ancient oaks stand witness,
cast shadows on the weir.
Rewilded fields feel larks' caress,
rising as a prayer.
Children listen to harmony,
forever lost to me.

Bees seen in humming flight,
ignore chemicals of shame.
Wildflowers are too numerous,

for admirals to name.
Insects awake to new refrain,
feel the softness of the rain.

Juniper trees flower untamed,
deserts bloom beneath their shade.
Returning from our wilderness,
as our fire sun starts to fade.
Real love enriches fertile soil,
new peace will not recoil.

Music of children's laughter,
warms our hearts like spring.
Threading joy through lifted mist.
silence has learnt to sing.
Let them hear a new world,
in the quiet I have made.

They mimic our blackbird and the wren,
sweet birdsong taught to them.
A little girl knows all the moths,
I'm learning how to see.
A boy runs wild in wolf packs,
how I wish it could be me.

Scotland's Wild West

Scotland's Wild West

As a Scot with many experiences of the wild but exciting Scottish countryside, the Autor's writings evoke many memories of the land which I had the pleasure of living in and hiking over in my younger days.

In more recent times, foot power has been replaced by horsepower but driving throughout Scotland still generates views which are difficult to find in many countries. The Author's poetry has captured the frequently changing and evolving seasons, plus the weather and wildlife that surrounds us. In the fields, on the water he takes our imagination into the heavens revealing that dot - which could have been a buzzard or was it an eagle? – one thing is certain, he captures and paints Scotland's life in words.

The locals talk of the characters, real and mythical, the wildlife, flora and fauna and local historical landmarks or past events with a passion and sentiment which the poet has captured, in his view of Scotland's Wild West.

From the Borders flocks to the Heilan' Coos and as far north as St Kilda, the Author's thoughts, descriptions in prose and his ability to describe the emotions and convey the atmosphere of Scotland, my homeland is making me look forward to my next trip to the land of the Unicorn.

John Ferris

HIGHLAND COO

Soft eyes peek through fringe of gold,
huge shoulder muscles never fold.
Heavy head, holds rampant horn,
a regal Scottish crown adorn.

Thick shaggy coat beats morning chill,
bravely graze wild glen and hill.
They wander belly deep in snow,
shivers never known to show.

Tough as old boots on snowy heath,
paw sparce ground for grass beneath.
See their snorts in lacy billows,
sharpest frost, no feather pillows.

Scottish Kings bold heraldic halls,
smoke-ingrained, black stoney walls.
Bedecked with shield and battered mace,
clan broadsword hangs in pride of place.

Draughty castles grey embers pile,
colder than a staked witch's smile.
Clan chiefs seated on granite rings,
strong leather capes for all their Kings.

Brave of heart, bold tempered steel,
highland cow will never kneel.

TAMMIE NORRIE

St Kilda awaits; with bated breath,
springtime arrivals thousands flock.
Puffins cover face, ledge and rock,
surely saved from their floating death.

Bird of beauty, bright rainbow beak,
designed to give that eel a tweak.
Nesting puffins' scrape burrows dug,
hidden from black hooded thug.

Children giggled, sang as they ran,
Tammie Norrie, silly old man.
On Kilda Isle they loved the clown,
gave him back his golden crown.

Rough seas heave on rolling swell,
huddled twitchers not so well.
Some found their courage in a nip,
or Qwells in their survival kit.

Puffin's master survival plan,
only one egg to rear and feed.
They never strain the Isle they need,
is it beyond the wit of man?

No Common Thing

Glide on thermals one mile high,
spot their prey or seek new mate.
Darkest raptor keen of eye,
long-winged harbinger of fate.

Oft seen afar in Scottish glen,
towered pines, demonic halls.
Many places devoid of men,
imperial flight, strident calls.

Watchers, huddled safe in their hide,
a slightest shiver, never still,
Ohs, aahs, buzzard hover, then glide,
majestic as she swoops to kill.

Heart will sing when seen on wing,
'common' buzzard?' no such thing.

Scottish Doe

Perked ears adorn three times the size,
nervously spooked by owl-like hoots.
Innocence mirrored in dark eyes,
feet in little black ankle boots.

Even grazing; on full alert,
head jerks up at softer tread.
Ears twitch, never can be still,
lives her life in timeless dread.

Those sloe-like eyes, softly aware,
there's no wolf or bear hunting there.
Safe from the alphas bloody lair,
no lifeless drag within that sphere.

Cull and deer hunt almost ceased,
their carbon footprint has increased.

NIGHT'S CANOPY

Night's canopy cradles infinity,
huddled together, eternal story.
Closer to spirit than we'll ever be,
see Scottish gloaming in fulsome glory.

Together, hand in hand, our love renewed,
adjusting our eyes to that awesome light.
Struck breathless at spectacular multitude,
we never imagined the stars so bright.

Was that a shooting star flared into view?
showered luminescent lights, sky to shore.
Incandescent glory shone diamond blue,
peers through from borrowed universe next door.

Starry, starry, night - darker hue,
Vincent alone could paint that view.

THE BALLARD OF BROCKEN SPECTRE

Two clans in everlasting war,
forever fought in Grampian heights.
Written into their Celtic lore,
those long forgotten hurtful sleights.

But young love will not be easily chained.
Rival Princess and Royal son ignore,
the dire warnings and potential pain.
As they lay together on forest floor.

Stolen time forgotten in each other's arms,
brave Beth and Finn ignore their hopeless plight.
Forest's scents soothed with alluring balm.
Scared, suddenly by distant shouts and light.

'Go now my darling,' young Finn implores.
be swift, I'll lead them off another way,
always remember, I'm forever yours,
both our deaths if you mean to stay'.

Evening awakens peaceful pace,
no stray light to stir dozing pines.
Choosing tread, velvet light in case,
dislodged needles betray the signs.

Every wary step danger fraught,
Scottish princess brave but scared.
No quarter spared if she is caught,
worries about the boy who cared.

Frantic, she is losing last light,
her father will be at the stream.
Wee slip of a girl but full of fight,
but they will never hear her scream.

Knew she had to make a stand,
no short sword, axe or shield.
Only a sturdy bough at hand,
prayed for strength enough to wield.

Light strayed across her homeward path,
spied Brocken spectre's misting fall.
Orange veil; she now caught her breath,
ethereal grey wolf stands so tall.

Chasing shadows sudden slowing,
kneeling, Beth bravely bends her head.
Meekly honouring alpha king,
as he loped forward, silent tread.

Gently nuzzled her offered chin,
whispered, 'Quick, Princess you must flee'.

Bemused, the voice was that of Finn.
She told herself, that cannot be

Breaking away, so fleet of foot,
branches slashing, cruel snagging sounds.
Behind, the pursuit much louder,
heard terrifying bay of hounds.

Bursting from the forest haven,
feeling wet heather; peaty loam.
Safe: sees ahead her father's men,
their lights and calls to guide her home.

Closer, views her family gathered,
sudden sickening, deadly blow.
Her tartan bodice blossoms red,
blind to bow but not the arrow.

Looking down upon her father,
silent scream betrays his pain.
As others begin to gather,
she's surprised to see her body lain.

Turns her head, and hears Finn's voice,
his wolf spirit entwines with her.
'Beth, oh Beth, we had no choice',
feels his power, she starts to stir.

Senses her inner wolf drawn near,
impossibly it must be Finn.
Alive and well she felt no fear,
she is dreaming, it can't be him?

Strangely, a smaller wolf now lies,
reflected in Finn's golden eyes.

FRIENDSHIP TRUE

She flowed across the purple glen,
fliting shadowy queen sublime.
Quick dart forward, then back again,
her truculent flock kept in line.

Slinks low keen pricked ears alert,
hears her Shepherd's calls and whistles.
Nips ewe's wayward heels to assert,
command amongst Scottish thistles.

Into yon pen, the last one in,
Tam, one more horizon to cross.
A rest for Beth, then go again.
homeward bound before daylight lost.

Quietly calls Beth to his side,
she looks up with adoring eyes.
The love she feels, she cannot hide,
he ruffles her fur, to muted cries.

He glances at his canine pal,
'one last pasture, keep on going'.
Gruffly; 'C'mon, let's go m'gal,
the weather's quickly closing in'.

He watches as she wheels away,
his heart so full of friendship true.
Couldn't explain if pressed to say,
he knows no words would ever do.

Was it love, disguised as duty,
that linked their telepathic mind?
Two hearts now beat in empathy,
their loving souls somehow bind.

One rare time in the hills they sought,
each other's warmth, in tempest storm.
Cocooned in snow and deep in thought,
my life for hers and be re-born.

ANGEL'S BREATH

Dark inky skies flee encroaching day,
sky's azure dome, painted by thoughtless youth.
Hear Nature's soft music; it's chorus play,
melodic echoes; nonchalant abuse.

Search life's forest of hidden pathways,
other travellers bind their fate to yours.
Fir trees tall, on centuries' display,
hope our own brief past, still endures.

My life, now bent as an ancient pine,
but as winds lend their voice to history.
Still have that wonder, oh, sweet child of mine,
be ever in awe of life's mystery.

A smile, sweet kiss, or small tender token,
in my misplaced hubris, soon forgotten.
Heady scent of angel's breath evoking,
some adored misty lover's daydream.

Gentle place, where distracted sea meets sky,
sea kelp, sardines, salt, shapeless sandy seas.
Soon forgotten floral fragrances sigh,
drawn from your lungs by fresh sea breeze.

Cool sea now invites; ankle deep and blessed,
remember those misty cathedral pines.
Was life such an impenetrable forest,
of lies, and actors who perform fake lines?

But pure sweet scent of angel's breath returns,
my mind tethers those once wild yesterdays.
Imploring my sad soul for what I yearn,
takes me gladly forward to death's own maze.

CROWN PRINCE RETURNS?

Sweet incensed forests welcome dawn,
hear antlers crack in combat winced.
Posing question, who'll sire that fawn,
while fair hinds need to be convinced.

This King who wears a crooked crown,
astride his mighty mountain Glen.
Old and weak should be hunted down,
to feed the pack, not sport for men.

Too many fawns, harsh cry is heard,
as Scottish herd is left unchecked.
Horned fauna, a carbon horror?
where is our regal warrior?

A savage chieftain stained in blood,
countless tributes we'll never raise.
No fanfare; skulking in a hood,
or brave introduction to our gaze?

Is a coronation promised once more,
will a Bonnie Prince return to our shores?

DWARFED BY MAJESTY

Underneath shapeless wings of dispersed sky,
lost, amongst slow shapes of vanquished light.
Devious lichen covered branches gentle sigh,
bids sad farewell to creatures of the light.

Dwarfed by dark majesty of the ancients,
needles dripping solemn sobriety.
Darker secretly scented excretions,
drapes stone altars of man's false deity.

Callous hoots of some nighttime warrior,
resplendent in entrails and bloody gore.
Hooded gold orbs reflect a savage scene,
as it's yellowed claw grips on a scream.

Whitened bones of life's lost unfortunates,
glowed cold relief of aged darkness.
Ethereal luminous invertebrates,
slow silver trails glisten in dark duress.

Lost lone sentinels of some bygone age,
sisterhood offers sweet peace sublime.
Retreats from smoky cobblestoned cage,
desperately yearns for another time.

A WALK IN EDEN

Beguiled; First stone style beckons start,
small granite sparks, capture shy sunlight.
Beaten track weaves through your joyful heart,
nature's avenues flee shrouded night.

Hills kneel before Scotland's pine canopy,
waterfalls tremble into trout-ringed pools.
Rivers awash with soulful therapy,
mend your heart with nature's jewels.

Floral tributes blend in tender cascade,
carpets of Corn Cockle offer sweet chill.
Primrose, Marsh Marigold delicate shade,
colour palette paints every heathered hill.

Shafts of sunlight witness a world apart,
vast seas of bluebells sway in passion throes.
Those unready, surprised with jolted heart,
even the chill winds are likely to doze.

Far removed from man's smoke-stained viaduct,
nature is more than water, stone and sand.
Be sure sweet rhythmic songbirds will abduct,
your cured soul to that distant promised land.

A Kiss – and Away

Soothing roar of dawn's soft decayed night,
sharp early breeze cuts a new-born day.
Awakened sky lends grey spectral light,
dreaded midges, unbalanced stay away.

No sea's roar, sand's grate – only a sigh,
nor wind-swept gull's morbid cries and calls.
Twisted notes of a broken cello string,
plucked as a demented Sea God falls.

Waves undulate, flotsam Lochside weed,
kiln-dried channel wrack crunched against rock.
Eyes search gannet dive, gulls' noisy greed,
sea scented senses, run amok.

Tanned, dark glasses, wild wind ruffled hair,
brace slippery rocks on sea wet slope.
Chosen spartan kit with delicate care,
surveyed sea; fly chosen with new hope.

Hardy rods sweep, pattern deft display,
crystal sea illuminates another world.
Fly dances, flickering trickster in play,
luminous, pearlescent beauty revealed.

Sudden ferocity, line ripped away,
screeching reel, rod bent almost double.
Brave sea trout, fought titanic struggle,
she lies on bankside, fought and lost the day.

An ingot of silvery blue beauty,
rosetta spots adorn her heaving flank.
No priest today; we've made a treaty,
kiss on fair bony head: hold, and away.

ARDNAMURCHAN LIGHTHOUSE

A lone sentinel stands against the storm,
surrounded, by cruel wind-blown enemy.
Gulls wheel on high, unearthly cry forlorn,
this tall hero still scans dark brooding sea.

Our most westerly point, vigilant still,
storm-embattled soldier rebuffs the squalls.
Honoured this VE Day on Scottish hill,
unconquered: so mighty island never falls.

Now at peace, surveys a new jamboree,
green gilets, telescopes and lighthouse tours.
No seafarers flounder all at sea,
now dolphins and whales roam our shores.

Too soon, hears sea's voice rant insane,
stands strong, saving sons of those before.
Beam of Life brighter than the darkest pain,
nurtures light on any distant shore.

Today's smooth waters herald the sail,
few cruel squalls or turbulence to tame,
No loin cloth, thorny crown, blood-red nail.
not Holy; but saves souls just the same.

No Cap in Hand

Found idyllic home with deer and raven,
no wall can protect their heavenly peace.
Wild eagles swoop towards safer haven,
tenant crofters clutch their cruellest lease.

Thrown down thirty pieces of US gold,
proud stolen heritage can't be replaced.
Precious liquid resources pumped and sold,
even their language became defaced.

They've fought against, and side by side,
through gritted teeth, gave their lives, their pain.
Couldn't stop or stem encroaching tide,
truly, a proud warrior race in chains.

Blessed are those fallen in foreign fields,
from far-off Scottish mountains forged and hewn.
Now, all their bloody wounds are healed,
weep for dying spirit of Brigadoon.

CASTLE OF SORROW

Ruined shape rises from mist covered climb,
watchful gulls wheel, but keep their distance.
Celtic Castle centuries out of time,
revengeful seas await another chance.

Reluctant shores shun any bracing squalls,
whispered entreaty angers windblown Mermen.
Defend lantern turreted moss strewn walls,
await haunted Chieftain's guilt-ridden clan.

Abandoned cruel thoughts; repairs lost pride,
vile treachery seeps ramparts of yore.
Blood-stained betrayal, as granddaughter cried,
still standing, Eilean Tioram weeps no more.

Reflections

Reflections

Those familiar with this poet from previous published work demonstrating his great love of wildlife, may be surprised by some of the poems on show here. These poems contain some memorable phrases, likely to resonate with many who read them.

The subjects covered are varied: from the perils facing young people nowadays *'Needle tracks hidden by a cardigan* (Howl at the Moon) and our lack of political leadership *'We blinked, and all the heroes are gone'* (A Chat with my Dad) - to tales of Native Americans' courage in battle or the historical persecution of those accused of witchcraft.

The author also draws upon the rich tapestry of his own life, with humorous stories and tales of love and heartbreak *'even the pen was too scared to write'* (Lady Scorpio) plus, an insight into night terrors and the darkness that lives in man's soul *'our dreams reflect where illusions die'* (False ego).

The poems in this section illustrate the many voices of this author, whether he has chosen to be analytical, playful or emotional. Taken together, they present a varied landscape of reflections on life.

Gordon Adams

Author of *To Write is Never Wrong*

WINDSWEPT LANES

I walk the windswept lanes,
meet fellow travellers who,
choose their attitude each day,
are judged by what they do.
They asked me to be myself,
in actions and what I say.

Live every day, as if your last,
you may pass this way again.
Learn from every friendship,
accept the joy and pain.
To guard against complacency,
to keep on asking 'Why?'

Opportunity knocks softly,
a problem in disguise.
Always act on a good idea,
and make your decision wise.
Avoid the negative advice,
stay positive and true.

Overnight success takes years,
through driving wind and hail.
Always face a difficult task,

as if impossible to fail.
Seek excellence, not perfection,
it's a balance not a race.

You can watch the street musicians,
wave to children on a bus.
Crouch and talk to that homeless hero,
one day it could be us.
Listen; don't take centre stage,
seek first to understand.

Breathe in the world around you,
let wonder lift your soul.
Hear the sweet blackbird's song,
don't let sorrow take its toll.
Learn names of flowers, trees and birds,
when in the **G**reat **O**ut-**D**oors.

Learn to love thy neighbour,
embrace their valued creed.
Remember their names and commit,
a secret kindly deed.
And, become that person who,
you'd like to meet in heaven.

L.A. Fires

The forest fires in Los Angles identified many fire-fighting heroes, as in many countries around the world – this poem is of a modern-day warrior knight.

They met at a bar late one night,
he needed shelter from the fight.
They sat together; souls entwined,
his soothing silence – the listening kind.

Head laid back and sighed his pain,
trying to quell the hurt inside.
Steely eyes had fought – and lost,
but never quit to count the cost.

Glowing jukebox played Johnny Cash,
black buckskin gloves stained by ash.
Clothes smelt of smoky smouldered pine,
his fire crew had just walked the line.

Burning hell and whipped Forest fires,
people's houses and ruined lives.
A hurt so deep behind the gaze,
he'd lost some brothers in the blaze.

Now Tim McGraw sings soft romance,
he held her closer as they danced.

A sway, a step, a graceful twirl,

for that magic moment she was a girl.

She noticed scars, in the neon light,

his soul bore deeper marks that night.

Felt his pain, could ask no more.

'I've got to go, my shifts at four'.

She whispered, 'Don't go - stay with me',

with that he let her hand fall free.

Said 'I can't', his eyes cast down,

'They need me, I can't let them down'.

She knew with all her heart and soul,

the latest fire would take its toll.

Seen his death behind his eyes,

but invincible spirit would never die.

HOWL AT THE MOON

Howl my sister, howl at your bitter moon,
surely sated when the cruel thirst is done.
Lucid dreams of sweet chemicals first kiss,
fly, fly, my darling, it's over too soon.
Needle tracks hidden by your cardigan,
not fooled by that dreaded opioid bliss.

Innocent laughter hooked up with the girls,
believed it was cool, turned out it was not.
False rebellion, now shorn of barricades,
breached, as her eternal battle unfurls.
Search for a dealer increasingly fraught,
because that last fix will certainly fade.

A heart-rending scene in that rancid squat,
parents sob, denied their hopes and dreams.
Her bloodied Uni bed, now left unmade,
weeping friends, their lives distraught.
They learnt nothing is truly what it seems,
no new yesterday was theirs to trade,

Charlie, Meow, Weed, Violin, Ket and Meth,
between her brain, needle and tourniquet.
Another life cruelly snuffed out at source,

why use such sweet names for a wicked death.
Once hooked, she can't awake and walk away,
dealer has dealt his final cards; Of course.

One small speck of humanity remains,
but pushers ensure she will never choose.
Parents offer their shelter with best intent,
broken promises won't ease their pain.
Can't give up the battle, or they will lose,
a child - God's one true blessing they've been lent.

FISHER OF MEN

I caught a fish
Or did the fish catch me
Stood by a river
Now I'm free

I chased a lass
Or did the lass chase me
Taught me to love
Then did flee

I caught a gal
Or she caught me
Stood at the altar
Oh, destiny

I loved a child
Or did the child love me
Stood by the cradle
We were three

I sought the truth
Or truth sought me
Burnt the lies
Inside of me

I found a god
Or did my god find me
Gave me faith
I lost foolishly

I caught the plague
Or did the plague catch me
Only in my grave
Did I really see

BROTHERS IN ARMS

I am stirred by the nobility and courage of the Native American people and their often brave but futile battle against all odds. Although I have never lived in their shoes, this poem is a homage to that bravery.

Ten steel-eyed noble Mohawk braves,

fresh shaven heads, tribe's war-paint daubed.

Half red, half black, their fate absorbed,

crazed look, but only souls to save.

Mohawks stand against one hundred,

bold brothers in death, as in life.

Mustangs whinny and prance in strife,

wild eyes roll back in fearful dread.

Sudden war-whoop for all to hear,

stooped low against their pony's mane.

One last look, eyes forward again,

a coward's death their only fear.

Warrior's death is wreathed in glory,

campfire dancers will sing their story.

A CHAT WITH MY DAD

Darkest days, where is the dawn?
They sell us our leaders, like our cars,
Lips move - hypocrisy and lies,
fake news leaves truth tattered and torn.
Facebook and X the media whores,
is it themselves or us they despise?

Mines in the jungle, rivers of blood,
desperate organised crime of life?
Presidential sycophants, PM's lair,
big business profit before neighbourhood.
Prey on the young, ignoring their strife,
learnt to chant but not how to care.

Overturning power, change is the trick,
sadly, change is more of the same.
Children groomed, dark social schism,
who's to blame – some hindsight heretic?
Politicians are well versed at this game,
no denial, covered up with an 'ism'.

Had this chat with my dad last night,
he says 'this bilge was forever known,
Our 'lads' would turn in their graves,

so be guided by truth's shining light.
If your being isn't turned to stone,
its surely, these kids you must save'.

Where are the Knights with dragons to slay,
powerful leaders not bribed, nor fooled.
Who won't stand-by on life's touchline,
and show commonsense, not feet of clay.
But even when their ardour is cooled,
they seize the day, don't wait for a sign.

Poets and authors write what you're told,
it's the age of celeb, phone-in the norm.
The power of truth is in the mighty pen,
but nobody's listening, doesn't fit the mold.
Solzhenitsyn, no more Siberian storm,
can't think, let's ask AI again.

It's cyclic, say those fools who'll scoff,
democracy what have you done?
The climate, land-rape and scourge,
can't stop the world if you want to get off.
We blinked and all the heroes are gone,
complacent madness, lunatics in charge.

WINDOW OF THE SOUL

My soul's window, blood diamond flawed.
hazy sunlight not always bright.
Kingfishers' orange refracted light,
discordant clouds cower, ignored.

Cold waterscape paints dark velveteen.
Skeletal witches' scorn oaken tree,
as Black Dog tries to silence me.
Failed grip slips in trembling stream.

Ethereal mist sees serenity shift,
regal swans, wear winter's white sails.
Nearer my God, nature avails,
silken webs are shaken adrift.

Sunlight breaks through resistant cloud,
directs bold shafts of light to play.
Thus, promises a much brighter day,
a pewter cross with a golden shroud.

LADY SCORPIO

When I started this letter to you,
even my pen was too scared to write.
Between the lines, buried from sight,
did my words have to cower anew?

My hand shook, our first touch reminisced,
was it cold fear or the longing pain,
that begged my heart to beat again,
and remembered that first sweet kiss.

She - beautiful, tall, but dangerous.
My joy was like a long-lost breeze,
whispering to silent cedar trees,
changing from gentle to cruel caress.

Scorpio, she said, as if somehow torn,
from what her dark heart harboured.
Scuttling terror revealed that cobalt armour,
hid beneath her naked scorn.

Filigree black silk snagged in motion,
on the carapace contained beneath.
A false word would soon unsheathe,
that toxic sting of sweet devotion.

Traced your shape in the empty space,
between my world and loneliness.
If I were a vixen, in life's wilderness,
I'd scream your name and scar my face.

We were meant to last for eternity.
Our love seemed eternal, forever young,
forged in the embers of a dying sun.
That vast space between stars and infinity.

But even as I write, I know,
that your cruel heart would only skewer me,
once again on your altar, when,
your mask would surely slip – again.

AN UNTAMED HEART

Remembered, still, your sleepy yawn,
lingered as shy, first rays of dawn.
Stolen daylight offered a place,
for your yearning heart's warm embrace.

Elegant, noble, nervous foal,
watchful caution, takes its toll.
Held your look, my eyes to show,
you're safe, my darling, nice and slow.

Willowy; skin of bronzed sunlight,
beautiful, but scared of cruel night.
Mirrors of your heart's soft echo,
forever sought a safe place to go.

Long lithe limbs, arms that held,
tanned slim legs that trembled,
with unconscious seduction,
at any softer silken caress.

She asked me, 'if I were an animal,
What would I be?'
I whispered, 'an untamed Palomino mare'.
Weeping, she softly touched my cheek.

Then carefree days, laughter in the rain,
tangled sheets and Dylan songs.
Wild, untamed; no intimacy untouched,
our drug of choice was love – and life.

Another fateful day unveiled,
when my soul's one act of betrayal,
shone through my treacherous eyes.
A silent scream heard in a fractured sigh.

Arrived home early, saw her note,
'You were my panther, but now,
I've felt your claws, and seen the abyss,
between your heart and mine'.

FALSE EGO

Much as a vampire has no reflection in a mirror –
some people have no self-awareness of who they are
and the damage they cause.

Each moment stretches out in time,

viscous in its tenuous hold.

Grey shadowed labyrinth, undefined,

wears a borrowed smile, so cold.

Broken hearts scattered to the wind,

regret not strewn against the rocks.

Callously never looked behind,

taken in by his golden locks.

Loves you've lost and loves you've gained,

dare not melt cruel ice within.

Broke their hearts, forgot their names,

lost his soul; and needs to sin.

See bloodied Vampire in his soul,

when he walks through a mirrored hall.

Looks back to view that gaping hole,

musing on his feverish thrall?

Our dreams reflect where illusions die,

whispering mirrors vanish, asking why?

BARBIE ON STEROIDS

'Better get a job my son,
you need to pull your weight.
Dave is looking for someone
you will need to make a date'.

Out I went with a flea in my ear,
no more girls, booze or skiving
Met my man Dave for a beer,
luckily, he was driving.

Turned up bright and early,
they sure saw the funny side.
Cos when I got my waders on,
they laughed until they cried.

We had to check the drain-aways,
from factories by the river.
Pouring dye, checking maps,
he made me watch and shiver.

Of course, I got quite cocky,
thought I knew the score.
Only Dave could mix the dye,
I was just allowed to pour.

One fateful August evening,
I received his frantic call.
'I'm too sick, won't come in,
you'll have to do it all'.

Through bloodshot half-closed eyes.
He brought me up to speed.
Told me how to mix the dye,
thought that's all I'd need.

Biked through the factory gates.
with red dye in dog-eared tin.
Swilling around the mixture,
I was ready to begin.

Mixed to Dave's instructions,
one part dye looked mighty thin.
Added 20 parts of water,
and poured whole lot in.

Checked the river outfall,
where the map was clearly marked,
Not a sign of colouring,
what a bloody lark.

Now I made the mixture,
the other way around.

Certainly, looked a lovely red,
sloshed the bugger down.

Once more to the outfall,
and much to my chagrin.
No red appeared at all,
why is this happening?

Wandered round the other side,
thinking through my plan.
The shocking vista I espied,
I felt a flaming clown.

Pink banks and foam so lush,
two Pink Ducks were annoyed.
Swans looking rather blush,
like Barbie on steroids.

Made myself scarce that day,
too shamed to see a soul.
Packed my bike and kit away,
and signed up for the dole.

Headlines read next morning,
'Oh, lovely global warming!'
Bold red type did implore,
Flamingos seen on the river Soar!

ZOMBIE SOUL

How to save a generation slain?
Oh, my sons, face shattered lives.
From that black prism curtained cage,
transformed a child with paralysed pain.
How can his innocence survive,
fuelled by our damned outrage?

Parents turn, look the other way,
Blind; as he climbs those creepy stairs.
Drawn to that dark web of hateful lies,
unaware of the price he'll pay.
Many are caught in that cruel snare,
Listen; to their broken-hearted cries.

How had that deadly fear increased,
abandoned within his darkened room?
Obsession hid the light of day,
what brewing hatred was unleashed.
Stirring him to stalk, troll and groom,
and treat young girls as common prey.

Does he feel the pain he's caused,
skewered by Zombie knives and Tate?
How can he ever hide his shame,

trapped by his demon's bloodied claws?
Feels it's foul simmering hate,
is this innocent child to blame?

Is he crazed with another's fame?
finale; with his mind unhinged.
Scary monsters now have flown.
leaving him with eternal pain
And the notoriety he's just binged,
of the friends he's never known.

A Second in Your Eyes

You are my August sun,
warm me before my day is done.

I see your eyes in a thousand stars,
erased my memory, healed my scars.

I hear you in the summer rain,
your laughter comes to me again.

The sweet scent of forest pine,
weaves within our hearts entwined.

I touch your lips, they imbue,
their softest snow-melt mountain dew.

Hold a second in your eyes.
Or tomorrow in your bliss.
Hold an hour in abandoned sighs.
Or eternity in your kiss.

WITCHES' BROOM

In Suffolk during the 1600's, evil lurked in the form of a man called Matthew Hopkins. He was the self-styled Witchfinder General, travelling from village to village playing on the superstitions and fears of the local people. They tortured, drowned and burned innocent women for no substantiated crimes.

Ghostly faces in decaying weed,
men bent against trusty steed,
lived also for their holy creed.
Wind rattled through shivering reed,
cruelly ruffled the roadside lake.
Stark reflection of the finders' stake.

Determined that a witch would die,
ducking stool never dry.
Kissed the girls and made them cry,
couldn't care if truth or lie.
Villagers stand resigned in shock,
quietly await the dreaded knock.

Dark satanic rites proclaimed,
souls and windows bear the stain.
Tortured sisters' betrayal claim,
ravens cawing devils' domain.
Pointing fingers of church and man,
Matthew Hopkins the charlatan.

Burnt them all to save their souls,
ensured the Church stayed in control.

WHAT ARE SHADOWS HIDING?

Happy in lost evening sun,
their lives between yours and mine.
Hiding from the night they shun,
glimpses of forgotten time.

Waits for a life forbidden,
in cruel blackness they take fright.
Shadows of shadows hidden,
weaved within their darkest night.

Let the moonlight wax and wane,
silver shafts will dance and play.
Quickly laughter turns insane,
when few clouds decide to stay.

As dawn breaks, they slide from sight,
dark is when they dare to play.
Sun awakes, be gone cruel night,
mirrored shadows of the day.

ENGLAND, MY ENGLAND

Search my soul for my lost England,
a greener land of worm-tilled soil.
Her skies painted with ancient spires.
neat hedges cobbed by unseen hand.
Farm's patchwork quilt of honest toil,
flocks of songbirds, treasured choirs.

We had those wonderous days of sun,
a time of innocence, youth and light.
In parks and fields, where families played,
picnic rugs, mum's best cakes - endless fun.
All happiness seemed ours by right,
took for granted, the freedom craved.

Clear crystal rivers to swim carefree,
chalk stream bubbled over gravel bed.
The summers warm, spring so sweet,
wildflowers worthy of the honeybee.
Saw Autumn leaves still not shed,
winter snow, no chilblained feet.

Our political elite took no stance,
sold our water and green Shires.
From on high, those fields unseen,

now paved with greed and circumstance.
Our patchwork quilt has now conspired,
to shroud our sacred village green.

Filth is strewn in stream and sea,
we now need sandbags by the door.
The 'shadow-men' drove the stake,
of greed that made our salmon flee.
Brave eagles flee and fly no more,
Excalibur, mired in a poisoned lake.

So, when our pleasant land is gone,
streets cobbled with yesterday's regards.
The corner shop, the leafy lanes, the mill.
only in memories will it linger on.
Old thatched cottages, unkempt churchyards,
overgrown with weeds and tombstones still.

LEANDER SPIRIT

A poem inspired by the Greek myth of a love story between Hero, Aphrodite's priestess who dwelt in a tower on Hellespont straight. On the opposite side was a mortal called Leander.

Dawn morning, breaks sacred silence,

sun is tentative, peeping child.

Gentle breeze embalms crisp and mild,

shrouded river awaits, intense.

Boat carried high on the shoulder,

brash Olympian swagger met.

Scull is launched; and riggers well set,

slide aboard, first strokes are bolder.

Lungs start to scorch many miles out,

pleasant heat doesn't hide the pain.

As oars sweep through the waves again,

above the wind he heard a shout.

Reverie broken, as into view,

was that her, in his fleeting sight?

If increased stroke rate, he just might,

sweep to his forbidden rendezvous.

Winter water now choppy and rough,
see the lantern, endure, endure.
Sets his sights for a different shore,
his giant strength perhaps not enough.

Huge back muscles crack from the strain,
striving, striving, softly bidden,
To Hero's ancient lantern hidden,
called to him through his increased pain.

She saw him, shyly waved each morn,
until her dreamlife fell apart.
Cast from bridge; by a broken heart,
her lifeless body gently borne.

Slumped over his oars, body heaves,
lungs and heartbeat exquisite fire.
Strung tighter than a piano wire,
tortured Leander spirit grieves.

Love transcends when even the Gods,
are saying no! - and stack the odds

BREATHE THROUGH THE PAIN

The following poem is my homage to one of the modern great poets – Bob Dylan.

Shadows falling; breathe through the pain.

dying light, never see it again.

It won't kill you, but it might set you free,

just to remind you of what you want to be.

Shadows are playing their craziest games,

light on the shutters, never seem the same.

Don't know if it's the hell where all love hides,

or in the darkness where your pain resides.

Morning awakes, driving hate deep inside,

walled in your soul, it's not easy to hide.

It won't be the Devil who's causing dread,

but playing guitar to a once empty bed.

Dawn breaks and embalms your fear,

eases the peace, you'll never get near.

No, it's not light yet,

but it's getting there.

Nightmares falling; screamed out her name,

been through the fire, burnt by the flame.

Cried for the many, cried for the few,
didn't hide from truth, it's not really you.

Ran through the streets, girls call out his name,
the scars on his soul seared by the fame.
Went down to Nazareth, and Galilee,
his song sheet nailed to a Joshua Tree.

Many he saved, pulled back from the brink,
eased the Hard Rains, won't let them sink.
Too many needed the needle and spoon,
cast out the dealers of his generation's ruin.

Met his revelation at an old country fair,
it's not light yet, but it's getting there.

WEEP FOR NOBILITY

In twilight shadows where proud eagles soar,
sacred spirits lament their mountain home.
Painted Lance prays at his ancestor's door,
pays tribute to generations unknown.

His Chieftain's daughter, graceful as a fawn,
is promised, betrothal strong and true.
Her laughter, like cool wind in the dawn,
he would be hers when green leaves renew.

Princess Dancing Moon, returned his love,
their union blessed by spirit and by man.
But this love would be tested from above,
noble hearts challenged, as only fate can.

A winter hunt ripped their world apart,
as a Grizzly's roar echoed through the wood.
Tested the mettle of a warrior's heart,
heard the white man's cry where cedars stood.

Though sworn enemies by blood and creed,
unerring arrow flew, and the great beast died.
White trapper lived, the tribe felt deceived,
Painted Lance, banished - 'Traitor they cried'.

Disowned beneath grey mournful skies,
through seasons past, wandered alone.
Harsh wilderness embraced him - until he died,
never allowed to return and atone.

Princess knelt at that ground so blessed,
drew her blade to end those lonely years.
into her heart a wicked knife she pressed,
to join her love in their ancestors' tears.

In legend, their love story still dwells,
where mountain winds through canyon tells,
of love that conquers exile and fear,
and hearts that hold each other dear.

Strings of My Kite

She looked so fragile in dawn's soft light,
holding her knees, on tangled sheets.
Naked, tanned shoulders shook and heaved.
Wanted to speak but my words took fright,
shrivelled dry at my first defeat.
Came to my arms, never dared to leave.

Standing in that room, spring days recalled,
carefree memories, oft wasted too soon.
Released my hold, but she begged me stay,
so, we still watched the bright stars fall,
illuminated the world's ceaseless gloom.
Held her heart and took her pain away.

She was the strings to my life's kite,
but she wanted those kite strings to sever.
Then we'd be in the stars – forever free.
She thumbed her nose, decided to fight,
laughed and cried, clung together,
made me more than I could ever be.

That moment always remembered,
she was strong from that first sign.
Letter box clacked, envelope unexpected.

Cruel words that left our dreams in embers,
shaking we both reached the line,
Dear Ms, please call, as we've detected...

Six months - the consultant said,
I was a hopeless, shattered shell.
Held her close on the train ride home,
but her heart didn't listen to her head.
Transported back from my lonely hell,
in this fight she was not alone.

We lived her bucket list in those few weeks,
never seen her shine so bright.
A ten-gallon barrel of memories filled,
eternally, they were ours to keep.
Her smile that made any darkness light,
and a spirit that wouldn't be stilled.

The fateful day came – she was gone.

Crushed by pain, I lost my way,
she came to me on a cool winter's eve,
whispered 'I lived for you – now you live for me'.

OUTBACK CHEROKEE

The Creative cruiser is my ex-sister-in-law Chrissie, self-styled Biker's barber, who tours the world, having adventures with Calamity Jane, her Indian Bike. The bike (a cut above a Harley) is over 650 pounds in weight, and the Biker-boys were astounded that 'such a little gal could hold that beast'! This story culminated in her stopping off in Olney after her 60-day European tour.

Creative cruiser swept into town,

sitting astride her Calamity Jane.

An Indian bike wearing a Cherokee crown,

all leather saddle bags, feathers and fame.

Successful women aren't always well behaved!

A powerful force of energy and drive.

Perplexing for the men they enslave,

knew one was here, when the Cruiser arrived.

Chrissie, fresh from her sixty-day tour,

glorious sight made all stand and stare.

Network with Euro-Bikers 'tout les jours',

biking, make-overs and cutting bloke's hair.

At every town, village or stop,

energy of a Titan, smile like the sun.

Out would come scissors, razor and strop,

even the French thought it was fun!

Star of the show on the Indian stand,
Calamity Jane pulled the bikers round.
She posed and preened for her Euro-fans,
love her looks? Then wait for the sound.

Watch Calamity as she wears her headdress,
dreams of war-horses in her distant past.
Patiently awaits her Cherokee Princess,
a new adventure, perhaps not the last.

Adorned in memories and a painted face,
Ex-husband's skull – appendages galore.
Pistols, sporrans, leather, no lace,
A few dints, a leak, but strong to the core.

With tears in our eyes and love in our heart,
we wave our brave warrior off to her flight.
But sometimes now, before our dreams start,
we hear Jane roar.

A SNOWFLAKE FOR UKRAINE

Each snowflake falls so differently,
hides what bled beneath.
Frozen images undefined,
ruined tanks and burnt belief.
A single rose: lone monument,
not wizened olive leaf.

Blown from another clinic burnt,
misshaped ash bemused.
Black wooden crosses: nothing learnt,
just soldiers being used.
Enemy drones see their trenches,
how can they be confused?

False Railway Children start anew,
Poor Petrov, Tanya, Serge.
Lucky Phyillis, Roberta and Peter,
never faced the soviet purge,
In darkest holes, lost children cower,
hear Wagner music surge.

Their tearful fear grows by the hour,
hear clatter of the boots.
They're herded into frightened pairs,

forced into stripey suits.
Faces press the carriage window,
the tsarist new recruits.

Will sun-lit cafes ever throng,
with children once again?
New Railway Children, didn't find,
a cosy little train.
Innocents bound to gulag hell,
cruel foster homes and pain.

Those snowflakes did fall differently,
truth, hidden from our fear.
Villages, towns - and freedom too,
scream to the world to hear! Beware!
They're hidden by a tainted shroud,
no Nation wants to wear.

FIVE CHILDREN A DAY

We lose five children a day, in the UK, to a totally treatable disease – suicide. The disease is real to the sufferers, even though we can't see it, like a broken limb or an open wound.

Looking for Monsters in your bed,

is a lesson in futility.

Nor dark rooms or cupboards bare,

we know with certainty,

There are no Monsters hidden there,

but locked inside your head.

There's a battle that no one sees,

comes from panic in the soul.

Only a C in maths, what's wrong?

All your friends got B's.

Leverage for a media troll,

to educate the throng.

Our sanity stands on the edge,

of the precipice called grief.

Or the cruel twisted knife of fate,

can't stand there on the ledge.

A cheat, a liar or a thief,

the truth will always wait.

Why does the search for Monsters end,

in the one place they can't stay?

We need to build a place to talk,

conversation with a friend.

We lose five children every day,

don't let the Monsters stalk.

Thank you for supporting

The RUR River Charity

ACKNOWLEDGEMENTS

My poetry book *Tears of the Wolf Moon* has been split into five separate but linked sections. I have been very lucky to have met people, whose literary minds I respect. They also did me the great honour of reading my poems and agreeing to write an introduction for each section.

I would like to thank Sue Upton (Author E M Tilstone), Terry Carter, David Carrington, Gordon Adams and John Ferris for their diligence and kind words.

My thanks also to my friends and fellow members of the Olney Writing Group for their help and forbearance. I endeavoured not to ruin their coffee mornings with a rendition of my latest rhyme.

I have received some thoughtful feedback from readers, which has helped me shape my thinking on the impacts of my writing – for that I will be forever grateful.

My lovely wife, Pat, has been my constant cheer leader, confidante, editor and hard-nosed critic. Her words have always been supportive but never too gentle!

And of course, my publisher Deb at BAA, without whom I'm sure I would be just another statistic.

About the Author

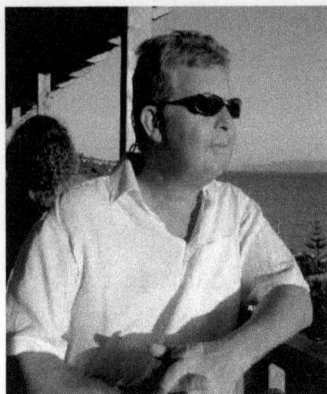

James spent the last fifteen years of his working life with two brilliant partners, running their own training and coaching company, T3 Web. His training style was shaped by more than twenty years in sales and marketing for BT and IBM, working with both large and small corporate clients. He was the first salesman in his company to graduate from Leeds University with separate diplomas in sales and marketing — an achievement he's still proud of today.

Despite this mainly technical background, James always carried deeper passions: the natural world, indigenous cultures, and reading. These interests had little room to grow during his corporate years, but they remained constant. When he joined the Olney Writing Group, something clicked. Surrounded by creativity, he found fresh inspiration and turned to poetry as a way to follow his heart.

He once heard that every writer has a single underlying emotion beneath their work. For him, that emotion is love — a love of the natural world. Its beauty and mystery have always pulled at him, urging him to understand and protect them. Over the last fifty years, the UK has lost around 20% of its plants and wildlife. Facts like these inspired his first poetry collection, *Animal Blues*, written to highlight the plight of our rivers and the creatures that depend on them. He focused on animals he feared his grandchildren may never see.

184

At first, he worried that his poems were too heavy, too tinged with warning. But a moment in a local bookshop changed that. A woman buying *Animal Blues* placed a hand on his arm and said, "I love your poems — they're from the heart. Just don't get too *poety*." Whether or not it was meant as a compliment, it encouraged him to keep writing honestly and not get tangled in the structures of contemporary poetry.

His new book, *Tears of the Wolf Moon*, still reflects his deep passion for the environment, but also branches into new themes and the questions they bring. He hopes he has continued to write from the heart, exploring each subject with sincerity and care.

Enjoy these poems with a glass in hand, in front of a warm fire on a cold winter's night.

.

Valued Feedback

I would love to know what you think of the poems within *The Tears of the Wolf Moon.*

Please scan the QR code using your smartphone to drop me a line, all feedback welcome!

Or email me at:

jim.coley2@btinternet.com

www.ingramcontent.com/pod-product-compliance
Lightning Source LLC
Chambersburg PA
CBHW031124020426
42333CB00012B/214